ISTANBUL
Insider's Travel Guide

HAMID ABEL

ISTANBUL INSIDER'S TRAVEL GUIDE

HAMID ABEL

Copyright © 2023 by *Hamid Abel*

All rights reserved. No part of this publication may be reproduced, stored or transmitted in any form or by any means, electronic, mechanical, photocopying, recording, scanning, or otherwise without written permission from the publisher. It is illegal to copy this book, post it to a website, or distribute it by any other means without permission.

First edition 2023

Published by *Knowvelty Press*

TABLE OF CONTENTS

INTRODUCTION 9

1.1 Welcome to Istanbul 9

1.2 Navigating Istanbul - GPS Coordinates: Your Digital Compass in the Maze of Marvels 11

1.3 Brief History of Istanbul: A Tapestry Woven with Time, Triumphs, and Tales 13

1.4 Getting Around: Navigating Istanbul's Tapestry with Finesse 16

ESSENTIAL INFORMATION 20

2.1 Climate and Weather: Istanbul's Symphony of Seasons 20

2.2 Local Customs and Etiquette: Navigating the Social Choreography of Istanbul 23

2.3 Currency and Banking: Navigating Istanbul's Treasure Troves with Lira Lore 27

2.4 Emergency Contacts: Istanbul's Guardian Angels in Times of Need 30

PLANNING YOUR STAY 34

3.1 Accommodation Guide: Where Dreams Meet Comfort in Istanbul's Embrace 34

3.1.1 Hotels with a View: Where Istanbul Unveils Its Skyline Symphony 38

3.1.2 Charming Boutique Stays: Cozy Corners of Istanbul's Soulful Tapestry 41

3.1.3 Budget-Friendly Options: Thrifty Havens in Istanbul's Welcoming Embrace 45

3.2 Transportation Tips: Navigating Istanbul's Tapestry of Transit 49

EXPLORING LANDMARKS   54

4.1 Sultanahmet: Where Time Travels Through Turquoise Minarets 54

4.1.1 Hagia Sophia - GPS Location: Navigating the Celestial Dome 58

4.1.2 Blue Mosque - GPS Location: Navigating Tranquility Amidst Six Minarets 62

4.1.3 Topkapi Palace - GPS Location: Navigating Royalty's Reverie 66

4.2.1 Istiklal Avenue - GPS Location: Navigating Istanbul's Cultural Artery 75

4.2.2 Taksim Square - GPS Location: Istanbul's Contemporary Crossroads 79

4.2.3 Galata Tower - GPS Location: Scaling the Spirals of Istanbul's Skyline 84

4.3 Kadikoy: The Bohemian Shore of Istanbul's Asian Heart 88

4.3.1 Moda District - GPS Location: Bohemian Bliss on the Asian Shore 93

4.3.2 Haydarpasa - GPS Location: Where History Echoes Across the Bosphorus 97

4.3.3 Kadikoy Market - GPS Location: Culinary Odyssey in the Heart of Kadikoy 102

THEMED ITINERARIES   107

5.1 Culinary Delights: A Feast for the Senses in Istanbul 107

5.2 Cultural Immersion: Unveiling Istanbul's Kaleidoscope of Traditions 111

5.3 Historical Marvels: Traversing the Epochs in Istanbul 116

5.4 Outdoor Adventures: Embracing Nature's Playground in Istanbul 120

SUSTAINABLE TRAVEL TIPS   126

6.1 Eco-Friendly Accommodations: Where Sustainability Meets Serenity 126

6.2 Responsible Dining Choices: Savoring Sustainability in Every Bite 131

6.3 Public Transportation Initiatives: Navigating Istanbul Sustainably 135

6.4 Community Engagement Opportunities: Embrace Istanbul's Heartbeat 140

LOCAL EVENTS CALENDAR 145

7.1 Festivals and Celebrations: Revelry in the Heart of Istanbul 145

7.2 Cultural Events: Unveiling Istanbul's Artistic Tapestry 149

7.3 Sporting Events: Istanbul's Arena of Athletic Excellence 154

7.4 Seasonal Highlights: Istanbul's Ever-Changing Splendor 159

USER-GENERATED CONTENT SECTION 164

8.1 Traveler Recommendations: Wisdom from Those Who Explored Istanbul 164

8.2 Featured Experiences: Istanbul Unveiled - Extraordinary Adventures Await 168

8.3 Insider Tips from Locals: Navigating Istanbul Like a Native 173

DAY-IN-THE-LIFE FEATURE 178

9.1 A Day Exploring Sultanahmet: Unveiling the Historic Heartbeat 178

9.2 A Local's Perspective in Beyoglu: Navigating the Soulful Streets 183

9.3 Kadikoy's Daily Rhythms: A Harmonious Tapestry of Culture and Community 189

9.4 Unique Daily Experiences in Different Neighborhoods: A Kaleidoscope of Istanbul's Charms 194

HIDDEN HISTORIES 199

10.2 Tales from the Past: Unveiling Istanbul's Historical Narratives 204

10.3 Unexplored Corners: Istanbul's Hidden Gems Beckon 208

10.4 Mysteries and Legends: Istanbul's Enigmatic Tapestry 213

PRACTICAL TIPS FOR TRAVELERS 219

11.1 Iconic Photo Spots: Framing Istanbul's Timeless Beauty 219

11.2 Capturing Local Life: Istanbul's Everyday Tapestry 224

11.3 Night Photography: Istanbul's Nocturnal Symphony 229

11.4 Seasonal Visual Delights: Istanbul's Ever-Changing Canvas 233

PRACTICAL TIPS FOR TRAVELERS 239

12.1 Language Tips: Unlocking the Melody of Turkish Communication 239

12.2 Safety Guidelines: Navigating Istanbul Securely 244

12.3 Internet and Connectivity: Navigating Istanbul in the Digital Age 248

APPENDIX 253

13.1 Useful Phrases: Your Key to Seamless Conversations in Istanbul 253

13.2 Maps and Navigation: Charting Your Course in Istanbul 258

13.3 Recommended Reading: A Literary Journey through Istanbul's Soul 262

13.4 Glossary of Local Terms: Decoding Istanbul's Linguistic Tapestry 267

1
INTRODUCTION

1.1 Welcome to Istanbul

Step into Istanbul, a city that weaves together the threads of tradition and modernity with the finesse of a master storyteller. As you cross the threshold into this vibrant metropolis, be prepared for a sensory feast that will leave an indelible mark on your travel experience.

Picture this: You're greeted by the heady aroma of rich Turkish coffee, mingling with the sweet notes of baklava wafting from a nearby café. Welcome to Istanbul, where the air itself carries the echoes of a thousand tales.

Nestled strategically between Europe and Asia, Instabul is a living, breathing bridge between cultures. The energy of the city pulses through its cobbled streets, adorned with the footprints of ancient civilizations and the vibrant hues of modern life.

Anecdote Alert: Legend has it that Istanbul was founded by King Byzas, who, guided by a prophetic dream, sought the perfect location for a new capital. We can only imagine his awe as he sailed into the golden-horned harbor, realizing he had discovered a city that would stand the test of time.

But what truly makes Istanbul a gem among global cities is its warm, welcoming spirit. The locals, with their genuine smiles and open hearts, are the true architects of your Istanbul experience. Prepare to be embraced by a culture that treasures hospitality as a sacred art.

Insider Insight: Don't be surprised if a shopkeeper invites you for tea or a friendly passerby shares their favorite hidden gem. Istanbul thrives on connections, and each encounter is an invitation to become part of its vibrant social fabric.

Your journey here is not just a vacation; it's an immersion into a living history book, where minarets touch the sky, and the Bosphorus Strait is the stage for a timeless performance. So, fellow traveler, as you stand on the threshold of Istanbul, open your heart to the city's symphony of sounds, tastes, and stories. Let the adventure begin, and may your time in Istanbul be as unforgettable as the city itself.

1.2 Navigating Istanbul - GPS Coordinates: Your Digital Compass in the Maze of Marvels

Lost? Fear not, intrepid explorer! In the enchanting labyrinth of Istanbul's streets, where the past meets the present at every turn, we've crafted your very own magic carpet – the GPS coordinates that will guide you through this living tapestry of history and culture.

Imagine this: You, armed with a smartphone and a sense of wanderlust, standing at the doorstep of Hagia Sophia (41.0082° N, 28.9795° E). The GPS coordinates are your secret code, unlocking the doors to an ancient world where empires rose and fell.

As you journey through the vibrant energy of Istiklal Avenue (41.0322° N, 28.9869° E), let the coordinates be your virtual companion. Picture the lively street, where the echoes of footsteps blend with the chatter of cafes and the rhythm of street musicians. Your GPS becomes a symphony conductor, leading you through this bustling melody of life.

Quirky Fact: Istiklal Avenue is not just a street; it's a living organism. Locals will tell you that every cobblestone has a tale to tell, and every storefront hides a secret.

Now, let's talk about the iconic Galata Tower (41.0256° N, 28.9744° E). Your GPS coordinates are your golden ticket to panoramic views that stretch from the Bosporus to the distant hills. It's not just a tower; it's a time-traveling elevator that lifts you above the city, revealing a skyline where minarets and modernity dance together.

Anecdote Alert: Rumor has it that Hezarfen Ahmet Celebi, a 17th-century Ottoman aviator, once soared from the Galata Tower with wings made of eagle feathers and silk. Your GPS adventure might not be as daring, but the view is just as breathtaking.

And for those who crave the unique charm of Kadikoy Market (40.9860° N, 29.0278° E), your coordinates lead you to a sensory wonderland. Follow them through the market's maze of colors, where spices perfume the air, and traders beckon with tales of flavors waiting to be discovered.

Insider Tip: When using the GPS to navigate Kadikoy Market, be prepared for delightful detours. The best kebabs and the juiciest fruits often hide in the corners not marked on traditional maps.

So, fellow wayfarer, let the GPS coordinates be your digital genie, granting wishes for an exploration filled with wonder, surprises, and the thrill of unveiling Istanbul's secrets. Your journey awaits – just follow the coordinates and let the magic unfold.

1.3 Brief History of Istanbul: A Tapestry Woven with Time, Triumphs, and Tales

Close your eyes for a moment and imagine standing at the crossroads of two continents, where the Bosphorus whispers the stories of empires long past. This is Istanbul, a city that breathes history, a living canvas upon which the hands of time have painted tales of conquest, cultural exchange, and resilience.

Picture this: The foundations of Istanbul, then known as Byzantium, were laid in 660 BCE by a brave king named Byzas. Legend has it that he was guided by a dream, leading him to a spot where the serenity of the Bosphorus met the grandeur of the Golden Horn. Little did he know, he was sowing the seeds of a city that would echo through the ages.

Fast forward to 330 CE, and Byzantium transformed into Constantinople under the rule of Emperor Constantine the Great. The city became the heartbeat of the Eastern Roman Empire, a jewel that sparkled with the Hagia Sophia (Holy Wisdom) - a testament to architectural brilliance and spiritual grandeur.

Fun Fact: Hagia Sophia has been a cathedral, a mosque, and now a museum. Imagine the walls whispering the prayers of emperors and sultans alike, a testament to Istanbul's ever-evolving identity.

The tides of time continued to ebb and flow, and in 1453, the Ottoman Empire under Sultan Mehmed II claimed Constantinople. The city's name changed, but its essence remained. The iconic Topkapi Palace became the seat of Ottoman power, and Istanbul witnessed the rise of the formidable Ottoman Empire.

Anecdote Alert: The Ottoman sultans, rulers of one of the most powerful empires in history, would stroll through the palace gardens, contemplating the city's skyline, their dreams as vast as the Bosporus itself.

Now, fast forward to the early 20th century – Istanbul became the heartbeat of modern Turkey. The city embraced a new era, where minarets touched the sky alongside skyscrapers, creating a skyline as diverse as its own people.

Quirky Detail: Did you know that Istanbul is the only city in the world straddling two continents? A ferry ride across the Bosphorus is not just a commute; it's a journey between Europe and Asia in the blink of an eye.

As you explore the city, let the echoes of these tales guide you through the layers of history beneath your feet. Istanbul is not just a city; it's a living, breathing chronicle, waiting for you to turn its pages and uncover the chapters that shaped its destiny. So, wanderer, step onto the cobbled streets and become part of the timeless narrative that is Istanbul.

1.4 Getting Around: Navigating Istanbul's Tapestry with Finesse

Welcome to Istanbul, a city that beckons exploration at every turn. Now that you've set foot in this enchanting metropolis, let's talk about how to weave through its intricate streets, where history and modernity dance side by side.

Imagine this: You, seated in a vintage tram, the rhythmic clatter of wheels harmonizing with the city's heartbeat. The tram glides down Istiklal Avenue, taking you on a nostalgic journey through time. This isn't just a ride; it's a poetic ballet of past and present.

Public Transportation Ballet:

Istanbul's public transport is a symphony of options. Hop on a sleek metro to zip across the city or catch a nostalgic tram for a leisurely glide through historic districts. The ferries, those graceful dancers on the

Bosphorus, seamlessly connect the European and Asian shores.

Anecdote Alert: The Istanbul tram has been ferrying passengers since 1869. As you sway with its gentle rhythm, you're sharing the ride with generations past, a link in a chain of time-traveling commuters.

Taxi Tales:

For those who crave a more intimate journey, Istanbul's yellow taxis are ready to spin tales of the city. Picture yourself winding through the labyrinthine streets, the driver regaling you with stories only locals know. Taxis here are more than vehicles; they're portals to hidden gems.

Quirky Detail: Taxi drivers in Istanbul aren't just navigators; they're custodians of city secrets. Don't hesitate to ask for their recommendations – you might discover a café or corner you won't find in any guidebook.

Ferry Feats:

A trip to Istanbul isn't complete without a Bosphorus ferry ride – the aquatic ballet of the city. Whether you're crossing continents or simply cruising for pleasure, the ferry is a floating stage showcasing Istanbul's panoramic beauty.

Insider Insight: Join the locals on a sunset ferry. The city's skyline transforms into a masterpiece painted in hues of gold and rose, a view that even the most eloquent words struggle to describe.

Walking Wonders:

For the intrepid explorer, Istanbul is a city best discovered on foot. Lace up your walking shoes and wander through Sultanahmet's historic lanes or the vibrant streets of Beyoglu. Each step is an invitation to discover the city's hidden gems and secret stories.

Fun Fact: The best Dondurma (Turkish ice cream) is often found at the end of an unexpected alley. Let your feet guide you, and your taste buds will thank you.

As you embark on your Istanbul adventure, let the city be your dance floor, and its transportation options your partners in this waltz through time and tradition. Whether by tram, taxi, ferry, or your own two feet, every journey in Istanbul is a chapter in the epic tale of your exploration. Enjoy the ride!

2

ESSENTIAL INFORMATION

2.1 Climate and Weather: Istanbul's Symphony of Seasons

Welcome to Istanbul, where the weather isn't just a conversation starter; it's a maestro orchestrating a symphony of seasons. As you plan your days in this city of contrasts, understanding the nuances of Istanbul's climate will be your compass for a perfect journey.

Imagine this: Spring arrives, painting the city in a kaleidoscope of blossoms. The tulips, Istanbul's proud ambassadors, burst into a riot of colors across parks and gardens. It's not just a season; it's a floral celebration, inviting you to join nature's jubilant parade.

Spring Serenade:

In April and May, Istanbul awakens from its winter slumber. The air is crisp, the sun is gentle, and the city bursts into life. Locals sip tea in outdoor cafes, and the

Bosphorus becomes a dazzling blue canvas under the gentle caress of the spring breeze.

Anecdote Alert: Legend has it that the tulip's journey to Istanbul began as a gift from the Ottoman Empire's ambassador to Vienna in the 16th century. Since then, every spring, Istanbul celebrates this gift with the Istanbul Tulip Festival.

Summer Sonata:

As the sun climbs higher in the sky, Istanbul's summer takes center stage. The days are long, and the evenings bring a lively buzz to the city. Beaches along the Marmara Sea beckon sunseekers, while rooftop bars offer panoramic views of a sun dipping into the horizon.

Quirky Detail: Seagulls become your summer companions. Whether you're strolling along the shores or sipping tea at a seaside café, these feathered residents are the city's unofficial tour guides.

Autumn Aria:

As the temperature gracefully descends, Istanbul unveils its autumn splendor. The city's parks, adorned with golden foliage, become an artist's palette. It's a time for leisurely walks through historic neighborhoods, where the air is infused with a nostalgic charm.

Insider Insight: Take a stroll in Gulhane Park during autumn. As the leaves crunch beneath your feet, you'll feel like a character in a timeless novel, surrounded by the city's history.

Winter Waltz:

Winter in Istanbul is a dance of contrasts. While the Bosphorus might shimmer under a light dusting of snow, the warmth of Turkish hospitality becomes even more pronounced. Picture yourself sipping Salep, a traditional winter drink, as you watch the snowfall from the comfort of a cozy café.

Fun Fact: Istanbul rarely sees heavy snowfall, but when it happens, the city transforms into a magical winter wonderland. Locals, usually not accustomed to the cold, bundle up, and the city takes on a serene, almost fairy-tale-like charm.

As you plan your journey through Istanbul, let the weather be your accomplice in creating unforgettable memories. From the vibrant hues of spring to the cozy embrace of winter, each season brings a unique melody to the city's weather symphony. Enjoy the show!

2.2 Local Customs and Etiquette: Navigating the Social Choreography of Istanbul

As you step into the cultural ballet of Istanbul, understanding the intricate dance of local customs and etiquette becomes your passport to genuine connections and immersive experiences. Picture it as learning the steps to a cherished dance, each move revealing a piece of the city's soul.

Imagine this: You, in the heart of Istanbul, greeted with warm smiles and invitations to share a cup of Turkish tea. It's not just a drink; it's an initiation into the art of hospitality that defines the city.

Tea Time Traditions:

In Istanbul, offering tea is more than a gesture; it's an extension of friendship. When invited to a local home or shop, accept the tea graciously – it's a bridge to meaningful conversations and shared laughter.

Anecdote Alert: Turkish tea is steeped in tradition, much like the leaves themselves. The tulip-shaped glasses and petite teaspoons are part of a ceremonial dance, a ritual of connection.

Gestures of Respect:

As you engage in conversations, remember that gestures speak louder than words. A slight nod of the head or a hand over the heart conveys respect and sincerity. The traditional hand-kiss is a gesture of utmost politeness, often seen in more formal settings.

Quirky Detail: The hand-kiss has its own etiquette. It's not just about the gesture; the timing and context matter. Engage in this timeless custom, and you'll find yourself part of Istanbul's living history.

Footwear Ballet:

Entering a home or mosque? The footwear ballet takes center stage. Remove your shoes before stepping indoors, respecting the sanctity of living spaces and places of worship. It's a dance of courtesy, leaving the outside world at the doorstep.

Insider Insight: When attending a traditional Turkish dinner (sofra), don't be surprised if you find yourself sitting on low cushions. It's not just about the seating; it's an invitation to a feast where conversations flow as freely as the food.

Respecting Ramadan Rhythms:

If your visit coincides with Ramadan, immerse yourself in the city's spiritual rhythm. During this holy month, respect the tradition of fasting by refraining from eating or drinking in public spaces during daylight hours. The evening Iftar meal, breaking the fast, is a communal celebration you won't want to miss.

Fun Fact: The call to prayer (Ezan) resonates through the city, marking the rhythm of daily life. Take a moment to appreciate this melody, a reminder that Istanbul's heartbeat is intertwined with its spiritual heritage.

Navigating Bazaars and Bargaining Ballet:

Entering the Grand Bazaar or Spice Bazaar? Prepare for the bargaining ballet. Haggling is not just a transaction; it's a time-honored tradition. Approach it with a smile, engage in friendly banter, and you'll find that even the art of negotiation is a dance of camaraderie.

Quirky Detail: Vendors often appreciate a bit of humor in the bargaining dance. Don't be afraid to share a laugh – it might just be the key to unlocking a hidden discount.

As you waltz through Istanbul's social tapestry, let the local customs and etiquette guide your steps. Each gesture, each shared cup of tea, is an invitation to connect with the soul of the city. So, join the dance, and let Istanbul's cultural choreography become a cherished part of your journey.

2.3 Currency and Banking: Navigating Istanbul's Treasure Troves with Lira Lore

Welcome to the city where the melody of commerce is played with Lira notes, each bill carrying a tale of transactions and traditions. As you navigate the markets and bazaars, understanding Istanbul's currency and banking system becomes your key to unlocking the treasures of this vibrant metropolis.

Imagine this: You, surrounded by the hustle and bustle of the Grand Bazaar, the air filled with the jingle of coins and the rustle of banknotes. The Lira, with its intricate designs, is not just currency; it's a canvas that tells the story of a nation's economic journey.

The Turkish Lira Waltz:

In Istanbul, the Turkish Lira (TRY) is the star of the financial show. As you exchange your currency for Lira, be prepared for a colorful spectacle. The banknotes feature iconic figures from Turkish history, making each transaction a mini history lesson.

Anecdote Alert: The Turkish Lira has gone through several transformations, much like the city itself. Today's banknotes showcase the faces of poets, scientists, and leaders who have left their mark on Turkey's cultural and political landscape.

Dancing with ATMs:

In a city that never sleeps, ATMs are your nocturnal dance partners, standing ready to waltz you through the choreography of cash withdrawal. Most ATMs accept major credit and debit cards, ensuring you're never out of step with your spending plans.

Insider Insight: Consider withdrawing a bit of cash for those charming street vendors or quaint local shops that might not accept cards. It's a chance to engage in a more personal form of financial dialogue.

Credit Card Tango:

Credit cards in Istanbul aren't just pieces of plastic; they're your companions in the shopping and dining tango. Most establishments, especially in tourist-friendly areas, readily accept major credit cards. It's a seamless experience, allowing you to indulge in the city's culinary and retail delights.

Quirky Detail: Some credit cards offer perks and discounts at popular attractions and restaurants. Check with your card provider – you might discover hidden treasures and save a few Lira along the way.

Currency Exchange Ballet:

The Grand Bazaar isn't just a shopping destination; it's a stage for the currency exchange ballet. Here, money changers perform the art of conversion with flair. Before engaging in this dance, compare rates and choose the partner that offers the most favorable tempo for your financial foxtrot.

Fun Fact: The Grand Bazaar has been a hub for commerce since 1461. As you exchange currency amidst its historic arches, you're participating in a tradition that spans centuries.

As you embark on your Istanbul adventure, let the Turkish Lira be your rhythmic companion, guiding you through the steps of local transactions and financial fables. Whether you're swaying with banknotes in the Grand Bazaar or gracefully using your credit card at a riverside café, each financial move is a chance to become part of Istanbul's economic folklore. So, cue the music, embrace the Lira lore, and let your financial journey in Istanbul be a dance of economic enchantment.

2.4 Emergency Contacts: Istanbul's Guardian Angels in Times of Need

In the heart of Istanbul's vibrant tapestry, it's essential to know that help is just a phone call away. Like guardian angels watching over the city, emergency contacts stand ready to assist. Let's explore this crucial chapter in your Istanbul adventure – a chapter where preparedness meets peace of mind.

Imagine this: You, surrounded by the historic architecture of Sultanahmet, suddenly in need of assistance. In that moment, the emergency contacts become your invisible allies, ready to swoop in and ensure your safety in this city of wonders.

Universal Magic Number: 112

Think of 112 as Istanbul's magic number – a universal summoner of help. Dial it for emergencies, and a network of medical, police, and fire services will respond promptly. This three-digit symphony is your lifeline, ensuring that no matter where you are in the city, help is just a call away.

Anecdote Alert: Legend has it that 112 is a number with a global passport. It's not just a number; it's a guardian code that transcends borders, ensuring that help speaks a language understood by all.

Police Presence: 155

Should you find yourself in need of the city's protectors, dial 155 for the police. Istanbul's law enforcement is committed to ensuring the safety of locals and visitors alike. From lost belongings to more serious matters, the police are your allies in navigating the city's challenges.

Quirky Detail: Istanbul's police force isn't just about maintaining order; they're often engaged in community outreach, ensuring that the city's residents feel a sense of security that goes beyond law enforcement.

Medical Marvels: 112 (Ambulance) and 110 (Fire Department)

For health-related emergencies, including medical assistance or fire emergencies, dial 112 or 110, respectively. These numbers unleash a network of ambulances and firefighters, ready to respond swiftly. Istanbul's medical facilities are equipped with modern technology and skilled professionals to address a spectrum of healthcare needs.

Fun Fact: Istanbul's emergency services aren't just responders; they're heroes with medical capes and firefighting armor. Their dedication to saving lives is a testament to the city's commitment to the well-being of its residents and visitors.

Consular Comfort: Your Embassy's Contact

While you're in Istanbul, your embassy is your anchor. Keep the contact information for your country's embassy or consulate in your back pocket. They are your guardians in a foreign land, providing assistance with lost passports, legal matters, and communication with loved ones back home.

Insider Insight: Embassies often have valuable resources for travelers, from safety advisories to local contacts.

Don't hesitate to reach out – they're there to ensure your stay is as smooth as possible.

As you explore Istanbul's enchanting streets, let the knowledge of these emergency contacts be your safety net. In this city where the old meets the new, these guardian angels stand ready to ensure that your adventure is not just memorable but also safe. So, keep these numbers close, and let the magic of Istanbul unfold with the comfort of knowing that help is always within reach.

3

PLANNING YOUR STAY

3.1 Accommodation Guide: Where Dreams Meet Comfort in Istanbul's Embrace

Welcome to Istanbul, where the city's hospitality unfolds like a tapestry, weaving together modern comfort and historic charm. Choosing the right accommodation is not just about where you rest your head; it's an integral part of your Istanbul narrative. Let's embark on this journey together – a quest for the perfect abode in a city that whispers tales of centuries past.

Picture this: You, stepping into a charming boutique hotel nestled in the heart of Sultanahmet. The scent of Ottoman-era spices lingers in the air, and the concierge welcomes you with a smile that echoes the warmth of Istanbul itself.

Grandeur on the Bosphorus: Luxury Hotels

For those seeking an opulent retreat, Istanbul's luxury hotels are architectural marvels. Imagine waking up to panoramic views of the Bosphorus from your suite, where every detail is a nod to both Ottoman extravagance and contemporary elegance.

Anecdote Alert: The iconic Pera Palace Hotel, a haunt of literary giants like Agatha Christie, offers not just accommodation but a portal to the city's glamorous past. Each room whispers tales of clandestine meetings and grand soirées.

Boutique Bliss in Sultanahmet: Hidden Gems

In the heart of Istanbul's historic district lies a treasure trove of boutique hotels. These charming establishments are like the city's best-kept secrets, each room a unique chapter in your travel story. Expect personalized service that goes beyond the ordinary – it's not just a stay; it's an immersion into the city's soul.

Quirky Detail: Some boutique hotels in Sultanahmet are converted Ottoman-era mansions. As you wander through the labyrinthine corridors, you're not just a guest; you're a time traveler, stepping into a bygone era.

Rooftop Revelry: Hotels with a View

Istanbul's skyline, with minarets piercing the sky, is a sight to behold. Choose a hotel with a rooftop terrace, and you'll witness the city's transformation from day to night. It's not just accommodation; it's a front-row seat to Istanbul's visual symphony.

Fun Fact: Some hotels offer panoramic views of both the European and Asian sides of Istanbul. Watching the sunset paint the Bosphorus in hues of pink and gold is an experience that transcends the ordinary.

Charming Residences: Homely Comfort

For a more intimate experience, consider staying in one of Istanbul's charming residences. These home-like accommodations offer a blend of comfort and authenticity. From cozy apartments in lively neighborhoods to historic houses turned into guesthouses, it's a chance to live like a local.

Insider Insight: Many historic residences have been tastefully restored to retain their original charm. Staying in one is like having a piece of Istanbul's history all to yourself.

Budget-Friendly Havens: Hostels and Guesthouses

Istanbul caters to every traveler, including those on a budget. Hostels and guesthouses are scattered across the city, offering affordability without compromising on comfort. It's not just a place to crash; it's a hub where fellow adventurers converge, sharing stories and tips.

Anecdote Alert: Some hostels organize guided walks and cultural events for guests. It's not just about saving money; it's an opportunity to forge connections and create memories with like-minded wanderers.

As you navigate the labyrinth of accommodation choices, let your preferences guide you. Whether you find solace in luxury, charm in boutiques, or camaraderie in budget-friendly havens, your stay in Istanbul is not just about accommodation; it's about finding your personal haven in a city that thrives on welcoming every kind of traveler. So, choose wisely, and let the magic of Istanbul unfold from the doorstep of your chosen abode.

3.1.1 Hotels with a View: Where Istanbul Unveils Its Skyline Symphony

In the heart of Istanbul, where the continents converge and the Bosphorus tells tales of timeless beauty, hotels with a view become not just accommodations but front-row seats to a visual symphony. Let's explore these elevated havens where the city's skyline dances with minarets, and every sunrise and sunset is a masterpiece painted across the horizon.

Imagine this: You, stepping onto the terrace of your hotel, the air alive with the call to prayer, as the sun dips behind the historic minarets. It's not just a room; it's a canvas where Istanbul unveils its most enchanting hues.

Palatial Opulence: Pera Palace Hotel

Pera Palace Hotel, an Istanbul icon, perches like a regal guardian overlooking the city. Nestled in the historic Pera district, this hotel is not just a stay; it's a journey through the annals of history. As you stand on its terrace, you're not just a guest; you're part of a legacy that has hosted kings, poets, and spies.

Anecdote Alert: Agatha Christie, inspired by the allure of Pera Palace, penned parts of "Murder on the Orient Express" within its walls. Your stay is a chance to immerse yourself in the mystique that fueled one of literature's greatest detectives.

Bosphorus Ballet: Ciragan Palace Kempinski Istanbul

Perched on the shores of the Bosphorus, Ciragan Palace Kempinski Istanbul is not just a hotel; it's a regal spectacle. Picture yourself sipping coffee on your private balcony as boats glide on the strait below. It's not just a room with a view; it's a front-row seat to the maritime ballet of Istanbul.

Quirky Detail: The hotel's infinity pool seems to merge with the Bosphorus, creating the illusion of swimming in the very waters that have shaped the city's destiny. It's not just a pool; it's a liquid bridge between continents.

European and Asian Embrace: Swissotel The Bosphorus

Swissotel, positioned like a guardian between Europe and Asia, offers not just a room with a view; it's a panorama that spans continents. The terrace unfolds a cinematic display of Istanbul's skyline, where modernity and tradition coalesce. It's not just a hotel; it's a rendezvous point for the city's two halves.

Fun Fact: The hotel's rooftop lounge, 16 Roof, is not just a bar; it's a celestial observatory. Sip on a cocktail as the lights of Istanbul twinkle below – it's a toast to the city's nocturnal allure.

Historic Elegance: Four Seasons Hotel Istanbul at Sultanahmet

A stone's throw from the Hagia Sophia, Four Seasons Hotel at Sultanahmet is a haven where history meets hospitality. The rooftop terrace is not just an extension of the hotel; it's a time-travel portal. As you gaze upon the iconic domes, it's not just a view; it's a communion with the whispers of empires.

Anecdote Alert: The hotel's courtyard was once an Ottoman prison garden. Today, it's a tranquil oasis where you're not just a guest; you're a custodian of the city's hidden histories.

Sunset Serenity: The Ritz-Carlton Istanbul

For a sunset spectacle that rivals dreams, The Ritz-Carlton Istanbul stands as a beacon on the banks of the Bosphorus. As the sun dips behind the city's silhouette, the hotel's terrace is not just a vantage point; it's a front-row ticket to nature's nightly masterpiece.

Insider Insight: The hotel's spa, with its panoramic windows, is not just a wellness retreat; it's a meditation space where you can rejuvenate with the city's skyline as your tranquil backdrop.

Choosing a hotel with a view in Istanbul is not just about accommodation; it's about framing your memories against a backdrop of breathtaking beauty. So, whether you opt for historic opulence, Bosphorus panoramas, or a skyline rendezvous, your stay is destined to be more than just a temporary abode. It's a celebration of Istanbul's eternal allure, where every window opens to a chapter of the city's captivating narrative.

3.1.2 Charming Boutique Stays: Cozy Corners of Istanbul's Soulful Tapestry

In the heart of Istanbul, where the city's heartbeat resonates through cobblestone streets, charming boutique stays emerge as hidden gems, waiting to cradle you in a blend of comfort and character. These accommodations aren't just places to lay your head; they are portals to Istanbul's intimate stories, where every room whispers tales of the past.

Picture this: You, stepping into a cozy lobby adorned with Ottoman-era artifacts, greeted by the owner who knows your name. It's not just a stay; it's an invitation to become part of a home away from home in the heart of Istanbul.

Historic Haven: Tomtom Suites

Tucked away in the historic district of Beyoglu, Tomtom Suites is not just a boutique hotel; it's a refuge where contemporary comfort meets Ottoman elegance. Each suite is a chapter in Istanbul's story, with a harmonious blend of modern amenities and vintage charm.

Anecdote Alert: The hotel's name pays homage to the Tomtom neighborhood's historic water cistern. Your stay is not just a night's rest; it's a pause in a district that once quenched the city's thirst.

Artistic Retreat: Georges Hotel Galata

For those seeking an artistic escape, Georges Hotel Galata is not just a stay; it's a canvas of creativity. Located in the bohemian Galata district, each room is a gallery featuring local artists. As you unwind amidst the vibrant decor, you're not just a guest; you're a patron of Istanbul's contemporary art scene.

Quirky Detail: The hotel's rooftop terrace isn't just an observation deck; it's a stage for the city's skyline to perform. Sip on a cocktail as the sun sets behind the iconic Galata Tower – it's a nightly show reserved for the hotel's fortunate guests.

Secret Garden Oasis: Ajwa Hotel Sultanahmet

Ajwa Hotel Sultanahmet is not just a boutique stay; it's a sanctuary nestled within the historic layers of Sultanahmet. The rooms, adorned with exquisite Turkish carpets and handcrafted furnishings, are not just spaces to sleep; they're cocoons of luxury, inviting you to immerse yourself in Ottoman opulence.

Fun Fact: The hotel's courtyard is a secret garden where you can savor traditional Turkish delights. It's not just a dining experience; it's a sensory journey through the city's culinary heritage.

Quaint Tranquility: The House Hotel Karakoy

In the midst of the buzzing Karakoy district, The House Hotel Karakoy is not just a place to stay; it's a haven of tranquility. Each room, with its tasteful decor and city views, is not just a temporary residence; it's an escape into Istanbul's modernity, wrapped in the embrace of a bygone era.

Insider Insight: The hotel's lobby isn't just a waiting area; it's a gallery showcasing local artists. Take a moment to appreciate the ever-changing exhibitions – it's an immersion into Istanbul's contemporary art scene.

Seaside Serenade: Vault Karakoy House Hotel

Vault Karakoy House Hotel, housed in a former bank, is not just a boutique stay; it's a testament to Istanbul's evolution. The rooms, with their arched windows and vintage charm, are not just accommodations; they're time capsules, preserving the city's banking legacy with a modern twist.

Anecdote Alert: The hotel's spa is located in the former bank vault. As you indulge in wellness rituals, you're not just pampering yourself; you're doing so in a space that once safeguarded the city's treasures.

Choosing a boutique stay in Istanbul is not just about finding a bed; it's about discovering a home where the city's spirit is woven into every fabric. So, whether you opt for historic elegance, artistic flair, or seaside serenity, your stay is destined to be more than a mere lodging. It's an intimate chapter in Istanbul's narrative, where each room is a page inviting you to linger a little longer in the city's timeless embrace.

3.1.3 Budget-Friendly Options: Thrifty Havens in Istanbul's Welcoming Embrace

In the mosaic of Istanbul's diverse accommodations, budget-friendly options emerge as thrifty havens for the savvy traveler. These establishments aren't just places to sleep; they are gateways to exploring the city without breaking the bank. Let's embark on a journey to discover cozy corners where affordability meets comfort in the heart of Istanbul.

Envision this: You, stepping into a vibrant hostel lobby, the atmosphere alive with the chatter of fellow adventurers. It's not just a budget stay; it's a communal hub where travelers share tales of exploration and friendship.

Hostel Harmony: Hush Hostel Lounge

Located in the vibrant Beyoglu district, Hush Hostel Lounge is not just a budget-friendly option; it's a social sanctuary for nomadic souls. The dormitories, adorned with eclectic art, are not just places to sleep; they're canvases reflecting the diversity of the city's visitors.

Anecdote Alert: The hostel's communal areas aren't just lounges; they're stages for impromptu jam sessions and cultural exchanges. Join in, and you might find yourself making music with newfound friends from around the globe.

Seaside Savings: Cheers Lighthouse

Cheers Lighthouse, situated near the Kadikoy ferry terminal, is not just a budget stay; it's a waterfront retreat. The dorm rooms, with views of the Marmara Sea, are not just sleeping quarters; they're windows to Istanbul's maritime charm.

Quirky Detail: The hostel's rooftop terrace isn't just an observation deck; it's a spot where you can enjoy a budget-friendly meal with panoramic views. Your dinner comes with a side of the city's twinkling lights.

Cultural Connection: Second Home Hostel

Second Home Hostel, nestled in the Sultanahmet area, is not just a budget-friendly option; it's a cultural hub. The dormitories, with their cozy bunk beds, are not just places to rest; they're launching pads for cultural immersion, connecting you with the city's historic soul.

Fun Fact: The hostel hosts regular events like Turkish tea nights and guided walks. It's not just a place to stay; it's a platform for forging connections and creating memories with fellow travelers.

Artistic Affordability: Bunk Taksim

Bunk Taksim, located in the bustling Taksim Square, is not just a budget-friendly stay; it's an artistic enclave. The dorm rooms, adorned with graffiti-style murals, are not just sleeping quarters; they're urban canvases reflecting the city's vibrant street art scene.

Insider Insight: The hostel's communal kitchen isn't just a cooking space; it's a melting pot where culinary enthusiasts from different corners of the world share recipes and create budget-friendly feasts.

Historic Hostel: Hettie Hotel

Nestled in the heart of Sultanahmet, Hettie Hotel is not just a budget-friendly stay; it's a historic haven. The rooms, with their charming simplicity, are not just accommodations; they're gateways to exploring the city's ancient treasures without straining your wallet.

Anecdote Alert: The hotel's common areas aren't just lounges; they're corners where you can find travel guides, maps, and tips from fellow budget-conscious explorers. It's not just a stay; it's a collaborative effort to make the most of Istanbul on a budget.

Choosing a budget-friendly option in Istanbul is not just about pinching pennies; it's about embracing the city's spirit of affordability without sacrificing comfort. So, whether you opt for hostel hopping or cozy dormitories with a view, your budget-friendly stay is destined to be more than a cost-effective choice. It's a chance to weave your own thrifty narrative into the fabric of Istanbul's welcoming embrace.

3.2 Transportation Tips: Navigating Istanbul's Tapestry of Transit

In the dynamic weave of Istanbul's urban tapestry, transportation isn't just a means of getting from point A to B; it's an adventure that unfolds amidst the city's bustling streets and meandering waterways. As you embark on this journey, let's delve into the captivating world of Istanbul's transportation – a mosaic of ferries, trams, and the rhythmic dance of the iconic yellow taxis.

Imagine this: You, standing at a bustling tram station, the air filled with the melody of street vendors and the distant call to prayer. It's not just a commute; it's a sensory immersion into the heartbeat of Istanbul.

1. Mastering the Tram Tango: A Dance Through Time

Istanbul's tram system is not just a mode of transportation; it's a journey through the city's past and present. The T1 line, winding through historic neighborhoods, is not just a track; it's a timeline of centuries, connecting landmarks like Sultanahmet Square and the Grand Bazaar.

Anecdote Alert: The tram's rhythmic clatter echoes through the streets like a nostalgic melody. Locals often say that riding the tram is not just a journey; it's a nod to the city's enduring spirit.

2. Ferry Fantasia: Sailing the Bosphorus

Boarding an Istanbul ferry is not just a ride; it's a maritime odyssey. The ferries, with their seagull companions, glide through the cerulean waters of the Bosphorus. As you stand on the deck, the city's skyline unfolds like a panoramic storybook.

Quirky Detail: Seagulls, the unofficial co-pilots of Istanbul's ferries, often accompany passengers on their journeys. It's not just a boat ride; it's a shared adventure with these feathered locals.

3. Taxi Tales: Yellow Cabs and City Charms

Hailing a yellow taxi in Istanbul is not just a transportation choice; it's a conversation with the city's charismatic streets. The drivers, with their friendly banter and local insights, are not just chauffeurs; they're storytellers, sharing anecdotes about hidden gems and historic corners.

Fun Fact: Istanbul's yellow taxis are not just vehicles; they're mobile art galleries. Some taxis feature intricate paintings and decorations, turning each ride into a visual experience.

4. Metro Marvels: Underground Explorations

Descending into Istanbul's metro system is not just a descent into tunnels; it's a journey beneath the city's surface, connecting diverse neighborhoods. The metro, with its efficient routes, is not just a means of transit; it's a subterranean thread weaving the fabric of Istanbul's modernity.

Insider Insight: Some metro stations are not just transit hubs; they're art installations. Keep an eye out for vibrant murals and sculptures that transform the stations into miniature galleries.

5. Walking Wonders: Strolling Through History

Exploring Istanbul on foot is not just a stroll; it's an intimate encounter with the city's living history. The narrow alleys of Sultanahmet, the lively streets of Beyoglu – each step is not just movement; it's a communion with the architectural poetry and cultural richness that define Istanbul.

Anecdote Alert: Locals often say that walking in Istanbul is not just an activity; it's a meditation. The rhythmic sounds of footsteps create a citywide symphony, resonating with the echoes of countless generations.

As you navigate Istanbul's transportation network, let each mode of transit be a chapter in your travel story. It's not just about reaching your destination; it's about savoring the journey and becoming part of the city's ceaseless motion. So, whether you're tram-traveling through time or ferry-floating on the Bosphorus, let

Istanbul's transportation be a thrilling part of your adventure – a choreography of movement in a city that never stands still.

4

EXPLORING LANDMARKS

4.1 Sultanahmet: Where Time Travels Through Turquoise Minarets

Welcome to Sultanahmet, Istanbul's radiant heart where the past and present converge in a dazzling dance of colors, sounds, and historical splendor. This district is not just a destination; it's a journey through the ages, where every step whispers tales of empires, sultans, and architectural marvels.

Envision this: You, standing in the shadow of the Hagia Sophia, the air imbued with the scent of Ottoman spices. Sultanahmet is not just a place; it's a living canvas where Istanbul's rich history unfolds with every passing moment.

1. The Grand Dame: Hagia Sophia

Hagia Sophia, a grand dame of architectural beauty, is not just a museum; it's a living testament to the city's resilience and transformation. The massive dome, adorned with golden mosaics, is not just a structure; it's a celestial portal inviting you to gaze into centuries of Byzantine and Ottoman legacies.

Anecdote Alert: Hagia Sophia's history is a tale of adaptation. Once a church, later a mosque, and now a museum, it's not just a building; it's a reflection of Istanbul's ability to embrace change while preserving its cultural essence.

2. Blue Splendor: The Sultan Ahmed Mosque (Blue Mosque)

The Blue Mosque, with its cascading domes and six minarets, is not just a place of worship; it's a symphony of blue tiles and delicate calligraphy. As you step inside, the serene atmosphere is not just a pause; it's an invitation to experience the spiritual grace of Ottoman architecture.

Quirky Detail: The Blue Mosque earned its nickname from the thousands of blue tiles adorning its interior. It's not just a mosque; it's a visual feast where the color blue becomes a metaphor for transcendence.

3. Timeless Beauty: Topkapi Palace

Topkapi Palace, perched overlooking the Bosphorus, is not just a palace; it's a treasury of Ottoman opulence. The Harem, with its intricate chambers, is not just a collection of rooms; it's a peek into the private lives of sultans and their concubines.

Fun Fact: Topkapi Palace's gardens aren't just landscapes; they're botanical wonders. The tulips, daffodils, and roses tell a floral tale, adding a burst of color to the palace's historical narrative.

4. The Lively Labyrinth: Grand Bazaar

The Grand Bazaar, a bustling maze of shops and stalls, is not just a market; it's a vibrant carnival of Turkish delights. The handwoven carpets, dazzling ceramics, and aromatic spices are not just products; they're treasures waiting to become a part of your Istanbul story.

Insider Insight: The Grand Bazaar's alleys aren't just passageways; they're time tunnels. Lose yourself amidst the stalls, and you might find that time, in Sultanahmet, has a way of playing hide-and-seek.

5. Meditative Moments: Sultanahmet Square

Sultanahmet Square, surrounded by monumental landmarks, is not just a square; it's a meeting point for cultures and civilizations. The Egyptian Obelisk, a gift from the Pharaohs, is not just an ancient monument; it's a sentinel witnessing the eons of human history.

Anecdote Alert: Sultanahmet Square is not just a gathering place; it's a stage for events and celebrations. Join the locals during festivals, and you might find yourself dancing to the rhythm of Istanbul's jubilant spirit.

6. Culinary Chronicles: Sultanahmet Eateries

Sultanahmet's eateries are not just restaurants; they're culinary time machines. The aroma of kebabs and baklava wafting through the air is not just a scent; it's an invitation to savor the flavors that have graced Ottoman tables for centuries.

Fun Fact: Some Sultanahmet restaurants aren't just dining spots; they're cultural ambassadors. Chefs often share stories behind traditional recipes, turning each meal into a culinary journey through time.

As you immerse yourself in Sultanahmet's enchanting embrace, remember that this district is not just a collection of landmarks; it's a tapestry woven with threads of history, culture, and the vibrant spirit of Istanbul. Every corner is an invitation to step into the city's narrative, where the past and present coexist in a harmonious dance, and where each moment becomes a brushstroke in the masterpiece that is Sultanahmet.

4.1.1 Hagia Sophia - GPS Location: Navigating the Celestial Dome

Embark on a celestial journey as we unravel the mysteries of Hagia Sophia, an architectural gem that transcends time and beckons travelers to witness the symphony of cultures within its hallowed walls. Follow the guiding coordinates to this celestial marvel, where history unfolds in the heart of Sultanahmet.

GPS Location: Hagia Sophia

Latitude: 41.0086° N

Longitude: 28.9797° E

Picture this: You, standing at the coordinates, gazing at the colossal dome of Hagia Sophia. It's not just a location; it's a portal to centuries past, where empires rose and fell, leaving behind a legacy etched in stone and mortar.

1. Celestial Gateway: Hagia Sophia's Historical Prelude

As you approach the coordinates, imagine the grandeur of Hagia Sophia revealing itself. The massive dome, an architectural marvel of its time, is not just a structure; it's a celestial gateway that has witnessed the ebb and flow of empires, from Byzantine glory to Ottoman magnificence.

Anecdote Alert: Hagia Sophia, originally built as a cathedral in 537 AD, later transformed into a mosque, and now a museum, is not just a building; it's a living testament to Istanbul's kaleidoscopic history.

2. Architectural Symphony: The Divine Dome

Standing beneath Hagia Sophia's dome, you're not just witnessing architecture; you're enveloped in a divine symphony of light and space. The celestial motifs on the dome's interior aren't just decorations; they're whispers of artistic genius, crafted by Byzantine architects who sought to touch the heavens.

Quirky Detail: The dome's acoustics are legendary. Clap your hands, and you'll hear the echoes reverberate like ethereal whispers. It's not just a dome; it's an acoustic marvel where sound dances through time.

3. Time-Traveling Windows: Mosaics of Majesty

Admire the mosaics that adorn Hagia Sophia's walls. Each piece is not just a mosaic; it's a pixel in a visual narrative that unfolds the stories of emperors, saints, and celestial beings. The mosaic of the Virgin Mary and Child is not just art; it's a glimpse into Byzantine devotion.

Fun Fact: Some mosaics were covered during the mosque era and later revealed during the museum restoration. It's not just uncovering history; it's a revelation that brings lost stories back to life.

4. Ottoman Elegance: Minbar and Mihrab

Explore the coordinates further, and you'll encounter the Ottoman additions – the intricately carved minbar and the mihrab. These elements aren't just architectural details; they're testaments to the harmonious coexistence of different cultural influences within Hagia Sophia's sacred space.

Insider Insight: The mihrab, indicating the direction of Mecca, and the minbar, a pulpit for sermons, are not just symbolic; they represent the seamless blend of Byzantine and Ottoman aesthetics.

5. Eternal Echoes: Imperial Galleries

Ascend to the imperial galleries, and you're not just climbing stairs; you're ascending through layers of time. The galleries, once reserved for emperors and their entourage, offer panoramic views of Hagia Sophia's celestial interior. It's not just an ascent; it's a journey into the echelons of imperial grandeur.

Anecdote Alert: Imagine the emperors, observing ceremonies and rituals from these galleries. It's not just a viewpoint; it's a front-row seat to history's unfolding drama.

As you stand at the GPS coordinates of Hagia Sophia, remember that this location is not just a point on a map; it's a pilgrimage to a living testament of Istanbul's enduring spirit. It's a celestial voyage through the ages, where the architecture speaks, mosaics whisper, and each step echoes with the footsteps of emperors, sultans, and the countless souls who have traversed the celestial dome of Hagia Sophia.

4.1.2 Blue Mosque - GPS Location: Navigating Tranquility Amidst Six Minarets

Embark on a journey to the harmonious intersection of faith and architecture with the Blue Mosque, an ethereal masterpiece that graces the skyline of Sultanahmet. Follow the coordinates to this sanctuary, where six minarets reach for the heavens, inviting you to explore the serenity of its celestial architecture.

GPS Location: Blue Mosque

Latitude: 41.0054° N

Longitude: 28.9760° E

Imagine this: You, standing at the coordinates, with the Blue Mosque unfurling its majestic domes and minarets before you. It's not just a location; it's an invitation to witness the celestial dance of Ottoman design in the heart of Istanbul.

1. Minarets to the Heavens: The Six-Towered Elegance

As you approach the coordinates, the Blue Mosque unveils its six minarets, not just as architectural elements but as celestial sentinels. These minarets, reaching toward the sky, are not just towers; they're beacons that guide you to the spiritual sanctuary within.

Anecdote Alert: The Blue Mosque's six minarets stirred historical whispers as they matched the number of minarets of the Grand Mosque in Mecca. It's not just a design choice; it's a testament to the ambition of the Ottoman architects.

2. Cerulean Symphony: The Exterior Facade

Gaze upon the exterior of the Blue Mosque, where the intricate blue tiles lend the mosque its name. The tiles, not just ornaments, are a cascade of cerulean hues that dance in the sunlight. The exterior isn't just a facade; it's a canvas of heavenly shades.

Quirky Detail: The blue tiles were crafted in the small town of Iznik, and each tile is not just a piece of art; it's a testament to the craftsmanship that has graced Istanbul for centuries.

3. Courtyard Conversations: The Abode of Tranquility

Enter the courtyard, not just an open space, but a sanctuary of tranquility. The courtyard's fountains, ablution stations, and greenery aren't just elements of design; they're invitations to pause and immerse yourself in the serenity that precedes your entrance into the mosque.

Fun Fact: The courtyard's fountains are not just decorative; they serve a practical purpose, offering a space for ablution before entering the mosque.

4. Spiritual Symphony: The Interior Grandeur

Step into the Blue Mosque's interior, where the grandeur isn't just architectural; it's a symphony of spiritual grace. The prayer area, adorned with intricate patterns and calligraphy, isn't just a space; it's a haven where light filters through stained glass windows, creating an ethereal ambiance.

Insider Insight: The interior's chandeliers aren't just sources of light; they're masterpieces of Ottoman craftsmanship. The interplay of light and crystal creates an otherworldly glow.

5. Ottoman Whispers: The Mihrab and Mimbar

Discover the mihrab and mimbar, not just as ornate fixtures, but as symbolic elements of Islamic worship. The mihrab, pointing towards Mecca, is not just a niche; it's a focal point for prayer. The mimbar, a pulpit for sermons, isn't just a raised platform; it's a space where spiritual guidance is imparted.

Anecdote Alert: The mimbar is not just a functional element; it's often adorned with intricate designs and calligraphy, showcasing the artistic flair of Ottoman craftsmanship.

6. Towering Ambition: The Domes Above

Gaze upon the domes that soar above the prayer hall, not just as architectural elements, but as celestial vaults that echo with the whispers of prayers. The main dome, flanked by semi-domes, is not just a structural marvel; it's a testament to the ambitious vision of Ottoman architects.

Fun Fact: The main dome is not just a physical centerpiece; it symbolizes the vastness of the celestial realm and the spiritual aspirations of worshipers.

Standing at the GPS coordinates of the Blue Mosque, you're not just at a location; you're at the threshold of a spiritual haven. The coordinates mark the gateway to an architectural symphony where every tile, dome, and minaret has a story to tell. As you traverse the celestial design of the Blue Mosque, may your journey be filled with a sense of awe and tranquility, as you become part of the eternal narrative woven within its cerulean embrace.

4.1.3 Topkapi Palace - GPS Location: Navigating Royalty's Reverie

Prepare to step into the opulent realm of sultans and concubines as you follow the coordinates to Topkapi Palace, an architectural masterpiece that whispers tales of imperial extravagance and Ottoman grandeur. Your journey awaits at the intersection of history and elegance in the heart of Sultanahmet.

GPS Location: Topkapi Palace

Latitude: 41.0115° N

Longitude: 28.9834° E

Visualize this: You, standing at the coordinates, with Topkapi Palace unveiling its majestic gates and domes before you. It's not just a location; it's a portal to the lavish lifestyle of Ottoman sultans and the secrets held within the palace walls.

1. Gates to Grandeur: The Imperial Entrance

Approaching the coordinates, the Imperial Gate of Topkapi Palace welcomes you, not just as an entrance but as a passage through time. The gate, adorned with intricate calligraphy and floral patterns, isn't just a portal; it's an announcement of the grandeur that awaits beyond.

Anecdote Alert: The Imperial Gate isn't just a decorative entrance; it served as a symbol of authority, where important announcements and proclamations were made to the public.

2. Courtyard Chronicles: The Divan Courtyard

Enter the Divan Courtyard, not just a space, but a theater of imperial decisions and courtly intrigue. The Divan, the administrative heart of the palace, isn't just a building; it's a place where ministers, officials, and advisors gathered to shape the destiny of the Ottoman Empire.

Quirky Detail: The Divan Courtyard isn't just an open area; it's a vantage point offering breathtaking views of the Bosphorus and the Golden Horn. It's where strategic decisions were made with a backdrop of Istanbul's maritime charm.

3. Royal Residences: The Harem

Venture into the Harem, not just a set of rooms, but a labyrinth of secrets and whispered conversations. The chambers of the concubines and the sultans aren't just spaces; they're witnesses to the private dramas and romances that unfolded within the palace walls.

Fun Fact: The Harem isn't just a place of confinement; it was a symbol of power and a showcase of the sultan's wealth. Each room is a chapter in the romantic and political sagas of the Ottoman Empire.

4. Treasures Untold: The Imperial Treasury

Explore the Imperial Treasury, not just a collection of valuables, but a trove of treasures that once adorned the sultans and their court. The Spoonmaker's Diamond and Topkapi Dagger aren't just artifacts; they're tales of intrigue, gifted rulers, and the opulence that defined the Ottoman court.

Insider Insight: The Imperial Treasury isn't just a museum display; it's a glimpse into the material wealth and cultural exchange that flourished during the Ottoman era.

5. Garden of Delights: The Sultan's Garden

Stroll through the Sultan's Garden, not just greenery, but a testament to the aesthetics that shaped the palace's exterior. The flowers, fountains, and cypress trees aren't just elements of landscaping; they're echoes of the paradise-like gardens described in Islamic literature.

Anecdote Alert: The Sultan's Garden isn't just a scenic spot; it served as a retreat for the sultans, a place to escape the rigors of courtly life and find solace in nature.

6. Café with a View: The Konyali Restaurant

Pause at the Konyali Restaurant, not just a dining spot, but a perch offering panoramic views of the Bosphorus. The Turkish delights and baklava aren't just desserts; they're treats that allow you to savor Istanbul's splendor while indulging in the palace's regal ambiance.

Fun Fact: The Konyali Restaurant isn't just a place to dine; it's a culinary experience that transports you to the opulent feasts enjoyed by Ottoman royalty.

Standing at the GPS coordinates of Topkapi Palace, you're not just at a location; you're at the crossroads of imperial history and architectural magnificence. The palace coordinates mark the threshold to a world where each gate, courtyard, and chamber tells a story of sultans and their courts. As you navigate the opulent halls and secret corners, may you feel the echoes of the Ottoman Empire's resplendent past and become part of the timeless narrative woven within the walls of Topkapi Palace.

4.2 Beyoglu: The Bohemian Beat of Istanbul's Soul

Step into the lively rhythm of Beyoglu, where the heartbeat of Istanbul pulses through vibrant streets, trendy boutiques, and historic landmarks. This district is not just a location; it's a kaleidoscope of culture, art, and the contemporary spirit that defines Istanbul's dynamic character.

Visualize this: You, standing at the entrance of Istiklal Avenue, the air alive with the chatter of locals and the melody of street musicians. Beyoglu isn't just a district; it's an open invitation to explore the eclectic and the avant-garde in the heart of Istanbul.

1. Avenue of Ambiance: Istiklal Avenue

Enter Istiklal Avenue, not just a street, but an artery that channels the vivacity of Beyoglu. The historic tram that traverses the avenue isn't just a mode of transport; it's a symbol of Istanbul's modernity, blending seamlessly with the pedestrian energy that surrounds it.

Anecdote Alert: Istiklal Avenue isn't just a shopping destination; it's a stage for cultural events and parades, reflecting the ever-evolving spirit of Beyoglu.

2. Architectural Elegance: The Galata Tower

Gaze upon the Galata Tower, not just a landmark, but a sentinel that has witnessed centuries of Istanbul's evolution. The panoramic views from the tower aren't just a sightseeing opportunity; they're a breathtaking journey across the city's skyline.

Fun Fact: The Galata Tower isn't just a historical structure; it was once used for astronomical observations and as a prison. It's a testament to Istanbul's multifaceted history.

3. Bohemian Bliss: Karakoy

Wander into Karakoy, not just a neighborhood, but a hub of bohemian charm and artistic expression. The street art adorning Karakoy's walls isn't just graffiti; it's a visual dialogue that adds an avant-garde flair to the district's character.

Quirky Detail: Karakoy's coffee shops aren't just places to sip your favorite brew; they're cultural sanctuaries where poets, writers, and artists gather to share ideas and inspirations.

4. Culinary Carousel: Galata Bridge

Cross the Galata Bridge, not just a crossing, but a culinary carnival suspended over the Golden Horn. The fishing enthusiasts on the lower deck aren't just anglers; they're part of a tradition that has defined the bridge's ambiance for generations.

Insider Insight: The restaurants on the upper deck of the Galata Bridge aren't just dining spots; they're vantage points where you can savor Istanbul's mesmerizing sunset while relishing the catch of the day.

5. Pera Palace: A Literary Legacy

Visit Pera Palace Hotel, not just an accommodation, but a living testament to literary history. The rooms, named after famous guests, aren't just spaces; they're chapters in a story that includes Agatha Christie penning 'Murder on the Orient Express' within these very walls.

Anecdote Alert: Pera Palace's Orient Bar isn't just a bar; it's a time capsule where you can sip a cocktail and imagine the whispers of diplomatic conversations and clandestine meetings that unfolded here.

6. Vintage Vibes: Cicek Pasaji (Flower Passage)

Explore Cicek Pasaji, not just a passage, but a vintage arcade that transports you to the Istanbul of a bygone era. The restaurants lining the passage aren't just eateries; they're gastronomic havens where you can indulge in classic Turkish dishes amidst a nostalgic ambiance.

Fun Fact: Cicek Pasaji, once a flower market, isn't just a venue for dining; it's a place where history and culinary delights converge, offering a unique blend of past and present.

Beyoglu is not just a district on the map; it's a living canvas where tradition and modernity coalesce, creating a vibrant mosaic of experiences. As you navigate its streets, may you feel the pulse of Istanbul's contemporary soul and discover the myriad stories that make Beyoglu a dynamic and ever-evolving chapter in the city's narrative.

4.2.1 Istiklal Avenue - GPS Location: Navigating Istanbul's Cultural Artery

Embark on a journey down the cultural heartbeat of Istanbul as you follow the coordinates to Istiklal Avenue. This bustling thoroughfare isn't just a street; it's an open-air stage where history, art, and the vibrant spirit of Beyoglu come alive in a captivating symphony.

GPS Location: Istiklal Avenue

Latitude: 41.0288° N

Longitude: 28.9737° E

Picture this: You, standing at the coordinates, the rhythmic sounds of street vendors and the distant hum of the historic tram. Istiklal Avenue isn't just a location; it's a lively boulevard where the pulse of Istanbul reverberates through the soles of your shoes.

1. Theatrical Prelude: Galata to Taksim Square

Begin your journey at the southern end, not just a starting point, but a theatrical prelude where the historic Galata district bids you farewell. The cobbled streets and colorful facades aren't just a backdrop; they're an overture to the artistic symphony that awaits.

Anecdote Alert: Istiklal Avenue was once a waterway during the Byzantine era, connecting the Golden Horn to the Sea of Marmara. It's not just a street; it's a historical echo of Istanbul's ever-changing landscape.

2. Eclectic Enclaves: Artistic Shopfronts

Stroll along Istiklal Avenue, not just a walk, but a visual feast where artistic shopfronts beckon with a kaleidoscope of colors. The boutiques, bookstores, and galleries aren't just commercial spaces; they're curated expressions of Istanbul's diverse arts and culture scene.

Quirky Detail: Some shopfronts aren't just displays; they're artistic installations. Street art and murals contribute to the vibrant atmosphere, turning Istiklal into an ever-evolving urban canvas.

3. Melodic Marvel: Street Performers

Pause to appreciate the street performers, not just entertainers, but maestros and artists who turn Istiklal into an open-air concert hall. The melodies of buskers and the harmonies of local bands aren't just background tunes; they're integral notes in the symphony of the avenue.

Fun Fact: Istiklal Avenue isn't just a shopping destination; it's a platform for emerging musicians. Iconic Turkish bands have their roots in the local music scene here.

4. Culinary Cadence: Gastronomic Gems

Indulge your taste buds in the gastronomic gems lining the avenue, not just eateries, but culinary adventures waiting to be discovered. The aroma of simit (Turkish sesame bread) and kebabs isn't just a scent; it's a sensory journey through Istanbul's rich street food culture.

Insider Insight: Some traditional lokantas (small restaurants) aren't just places to eat; they're time capsules where recipes have been passed down through generations, creating a symphony of flavors.

5. Historic Harmony: St. Anthony of Padua Church

Marvel at the St. Anthony of Padua Church, not just a religious site, but a historic landmark that adds a harmonious note to Istiklal's cultural tapestry. The church's neo-Gothic architecture and iconic bell tower aren't just structures; they're reminders of Istanbul's diverse religious heritage.

Anecdote Alert: The church isn't just a place of worship; it played a role in Istanbul's cultural evolution. The first Turkish language opera in the Ottoman Empire premiered here.

6. Nighttime Crescendo: The Avenue After Dark

Experience Istiklal Avenue after sunset, not just an evening stroll, but a nighttime crescendo where the neon lights and bustling nightlife transform the atmosphere. The bars, clubs, and theaters aren't just venues; they're stages that invite you to be part of Istanbul's nocturnal allure.

Fun Fact: The historic tram isn't just a daytime feature; it continues its rhythmic journey into the night, adding a touch of nostalgia to the evening ambiance.

As you traverse Istiklal Avenue, remember that this isn't just a walk; it's a cultural pilgrimage. The coordinates mark the entry point to a living, breathing artery of Istanbul, where each step is a dance, and every storefront is a chapter in the city's vibrant narrative. May your journey along Istiklal be filled with the lively echoes of Istanbul's past and the contemporary rhythm that defines its pulsating present.

4.2.2 Taksim Square - GPS Location: Istanbul's Contemporary Crossroads

Embark on an urban odyssey as you follow the coordinates to Taksim Square, the contemporary crossroads of Istanbul. This bustling square isn't just a geographic point; it's a vibrant nucleus where culture, politics, and the heartbeat of the city converge in a dynamic dance.

GPS Location: Taksim Square

Latitude: 41.0369° N

Longitude: 28.9862° E

Imagine this: You, standing at the coordinates, with Taksim Square unfolding before you like an open stage. The bustle of people, the distant sounds of street vendors—it's not just a location; it's a dynamic spectacle where Istanbul's modern spirit takes center stage.

1. Republic Monument: The Sentinel of Independence

Commence your journey at the Republic Monument, not just a sculpture, but a sentinel that guards the ideals of the Turkish Republic. The statues symbolizing courage and sacrifice aren't just bronze figures; they're a visual anthem to the nation's history.

Anecdote Alert: The Republic Monument isn't just a memorial; it witnessed significant events, including the proclamation of the Turkish Republic in 1923. It stands as a silent witness to the nation's journey.

2. Gezi Park: A Green Oasis

Explore the verdant haven of Gezi Park, not just a park, but a lush escape from the urban rhythm. The trees, flowers, and tranquil pathways aren't just elements of landscaping; they're an invitation to pause, breathe, and absorb the green oasis amidst the urban sprawl.

Quirky Detail: Gezi Park isn't just a recreational space; it played a pivotal role in the 2013 protests, becoming a symbol of civic engagement and the city's collective voice.

3. Cultural Melting Pot: Istiklal Street's Extension

Venture along Istiklal Street's extension leading to Taksim Square, not just a continuation, but a boulevard that mirrors the cultural vibrancy of Beyoglu. The shops, cafes, and theaters aren't just extensions; they're threads woven into the tapestry of Istanbul's contemporary narrative.

Fun Fact: Istiklal Street's extension isn't just a commercial stretch; it hosts numerous cultural events, street performances, and parades, turning Taksim Square into a cultural melting pot.

4. Beyoglu Clock Tower: A Timeless Icon

Admire the Beyoglu Clock Tower, not just a timepiece, but a symbolic icon that has marked the passing hours since the late 19th century. The clock faces, not just markers of time; they're witness to the changing landscape of Taksim Square and the city beyond.

Insider Insight: The Beyoglu Clock Tower isn't just a practical structure; it was a gift from the German Emperor Wilhelm II. It's a testament to the historical connections between Germany and the Ottoman Empire.

5. Pulsating Nightlife: Taksim After Dark

Experience Taksim Square after sunset, not just a transition, but a metamorphosis into a nocturnal realm where the square's energy takes on a different hue. The illuminated facades, vibrant cafes, and buzzing nightlife venues aren't just nocturnal fixtures; they're ingredients that flavor Taksim's dynamic after-dark ambiance.

Anecdote Alert: Taksim's nightlife isn't just about bars and clubs; it's a cultural amalgamation where locals and tourists alike come together to revel in the city's diverse entertainment scene.

6. Metro Entrance: The Underground Gateway

Descend into the metro station, not just an entrance, but an underground gateway connecting Taksim Square to the city's vast transportation network. The comings and goings of commuters aren't just movements; they're a testament to Istanbul's ceaseless urban rhythm.

Fun Fact: The Taksim Metro Entrance isn't just a transit point; it's a contemporary architectural marvel designed by the renowned architect Aytac Architects.

Standing at the GPS coordinates of Taksim Square, you're not just at a location; you're at the heart of Istanbul's modern narrative. The coordinates mark the meeting point of history, culture, and the city's ever-evolving spirit. As you navigate the dynamic rhythm of Taksim Square, may you feel the pulse of Istanbul's contemporary soul, where tradition and modernity dance in harmony, creating a tapestry of experiences unique to this vibrant urban center.

4.2.3 Galata Tower - GPS Location: Scaling the Spirals of Istanbul's Skyline

Embark on an ascent through history and panoramic vistas as you follow the coordinates to Galata Tower, an iconic landmark that graces Istanbul's skyline. This medieval marvel isn't just a structure; it's a spiraling testament to the city's rich past and breathtaking present.

GPS Location: Galata Tower

Latitude: 41.0259° N

Longitude: 28.9744° E

Imagine this: You, standing at the coordinates, with Galata Tower soaring above you, a sentinel overlooking the city. The bustling streets below, the Bosphorus stretching into the horizon—it's not just a location; it's a vertical journey through Istanbul's layers of time.

1. Medieval Sentinel: Galata's Historical Vigil

Commence your journey at Galata Tower, not just a tower, but a medieval sentinel that has watched over Istanbul for centuries. The cylindrical silhouette and stone façade aren't just architectural elements; they're guardians of the city's historical narrative.

Anecdote Alert: Galata Tower, originally known as the Tower of Christ, isn't just a structure; it has served as a watchtower, fire lookout, and even a prison throughout its diverse history.

2. Spiral Ascent: A Staircase Through Time

Ascend the spiral staircase, not just steps, but a journey through the annals of Istanbul's past. The narrow corridors and occasional windows aren't just architectural features; they're glimpses into the city's evolution as you climb higher toward the panoramic summit.

Quirky Detail: The spiral staircase isn't just a functional element; it's a strategic design that allowed defenders to navigate quickly while maintaining a defensive position.

3. Breathtaking Panorama: Istanbul's Tapestry Below

Reach the observation deck, not just a vantage point, but a breathtaking perch that unveils Istanbul's sprawling tapestry. The domes of Hagia Sophia, the minarets of the Blue Mosque, and the shimmering waters of the Bosphorus aren't just views; they're living panoramas that stretch from Europe to Asia.

Fun Fact: The observation deck isn't just for sightseeing; it has been a venue for various events, from scientific experiments to extravagant celebrations.

4. Twilight Magic: Galata After Sunset

Experience Galata Tower after sunset, not just a transition, but a transformation into a magical realm where the city lights begin to twinkle. The evening ambiance, the city awash in hues of orange and blue, isn't just a nightly occurrence; it's a celestial spectacle that enchants every visitor.

Insider Insight: The Galata Tower isn't just a landmark during the day; it becomes a beacon at night, visible from various parts of Istanbul, adding a touch of mystique to the city's skyline.

5. Culinary Soirée: The Tower's Restaurants

Dine at the restaurants surrounding Galata Tower, not just eateries, but culinary venues that offer delectable dishes with a side of panoramic views. The cuisine, a fusion of Turkish delights and international flavors, isn't just a meal; it's an experience that combines gastronomy with the allure of the tower's ambiance.

Anecdote Alert: Galata Tower's restaurants aren't just modern additions; they echo the historical tradition of towers being utilized as social spaces, where communities gathered for both sustenance and camaraderie.

6. Tower Tales: Legends and Local Lore

Immerse yourself in the legends surrounding Galata Tower, not just stories, but a tapestry of local lore that adds layers to the tower's mystique. The tale of Hezarfen Ahmet Celebi, who purportedly glided from the tower in the 17th century, isn't just a legend; it's a testament to the human fascination with flight and freedom.

Fun Fact: Galata Tower isn't just a static monument; it has been featured in numerous works of literature, poetry, and art, becoming a muse for creators throughout the ages.

Standing at the GPS coordinates of Galata Tower, you're not just at a location; you're at the summit of Istanbul's historical and visual grandeur. The coordinates mark the gateway to a vertical journey through time, where each step echoes with the footsteps of centuries past. May your ascent be filled with awe, and the panoramic embrace of Galata Tower become a cherished memory, etched into your personal narrative of Istanbul's enchanting skyline.

4.3 Kadikoy: The Bohemian Shore of Istanbul's Asian Heart

Cross the Bosphorus and step into the vibrant heartbeat of Kadikoy, an Asian gem that pulsates with energy, culture, and the unmistakable rhythm of Istanbul's Anatolian soul. This district isn't just a destination; it's a living canvas where history, contemporary flair, and the allure of the Bosphorus converge.

Visualize this: You, stepping off the ferry onto Kadikoy's bustling waterfront, the aroma of street food wafting through the air, the lively chatter of locals—it's not just a location; it's an immersive journey into the Asian side's dynamic spirit.

1. Ferry Arrival: The Gateway to Kadikoy

Begin your Kadikoy adventure with a ferry ride, not just a transportation mode, but a scenic voyage that offers unrivaled views of Istanbul's European and Asian shores. The seagulls accompanying the ferry aren't just birds; they're your welcoming committee to Kadikoy's bustling shores.

Anecdote Alert: The ferry ride to Kadikoy isn't just a means of transport; it's a quintessential Istanbul experience. The seafaring tradition echoes the city's historical reliance on maritime routes.

2. Moda: A Bohemian Retreat

Explore the Moda neighborhood, not just a district, but a bohemian retreat with tree-lined streets, charming cafes, and a laid-back ambiance. The vintage boutiques and second-hand bookstores aren't just shops; they're windows into Moda's eclectic character.

Quirky Detail: Moda isn't just a residential area; it's a haven for artists and writers. The streets are adorned with street art and murals, reflecting the neighborhood's creative spirit.

3. Street Bazaars: Market Melodies

Wander through Kadikoy's vibrant street bazaars, not just markets, but lively theaters of commerce where vendors hawk their wares with flair. The colors of fresh produce, the aroma of spices, and the bargaining banter aren't just market scenes; they're sensory symphonies that define Kadikoy's authenticity.

Fun Fact: The street bazaars aren't just places to buy goods; they are social hubs where locals gather, exchange stories, and share the warmth of Anatolian hospitality.

4. Historic Landmarks: Haydarpasa and Bull Statue

Marvel at the historic Haydarpasa Railway Station, not just a station, but an architectural masterpiece that echoes the city's railway legacy. The iconic Bull Statue nearby isn't just public art; it's a symbol of Kadikoy's resilience and strength.

Insider Insight: Haydarpasa isn't just a train station; it has witnessed historical events, including being a hospital during World War I and a significant transport hub.

5. Gastronomic Galore: Kadikoy's Culinary Delights

Indulge in Kadikoy's culinary scene, not just a meal, but a gastronomic adventure through traditional Turkish dishes and international flavors. The seafood restaurants along the waterfront aren't just eateries; they're panoramic dining venues where you can savor the catch of the day with a view of the Bosphorus.

Anecdote Alert: Kadikoy's culinary scene isn't just about food; it's a fusion of diverse influences, reflecting the city's history as a melting pot of cultures.

6. Cultural Haven: Kadikoy's Theaters and Arts Scene

Immerse yourself in Kadikoy's arts scene, not just cultural venues, but theaters and galleries that showcase the district's creative spirit. The performances at Sureyya Opera House aren't just shows; they're cultural expressions that resonate with Kadikoy's artistic heartbeat.

Fun Fact: Kadikoy's cultural scene isn't just contemporary; it has deep historical roots. The Sureyya Opera House, dating back to the early 20th century, is an architectural gem.

Kadikoy is not just a district across the Bosphorus; it's a dynamic enclave that captures the essence of Istanbul's Asian soul. As you explore its streets, indulge in its culinary delights, and soak in its cultural ambiance, may Kadikoy become a vibrant chapter in your Istanbul adventure, where the cadence of Anatolian life harmonizes with the timeless allure of the Bosphorus.

4.3.1 Moda District - GPS Location: Bohemian Bliss on the Asian Shore

Embark on a journey through the enchanting streets of Moda, a district that defines bohemian charm on Istanbul's Asian side. Follow the coordinates to discover a neighborhood where tree-lined avenues, eclectic boutiques, and the timeless Bosphorus breeze create a tapestry of creativity and laid-back elegance.

GPS Location: Moda District

Latitude: 40.9905° N

Longitude: 29.0270° E

Visualize this: You, standing at the coordinates, surrounded by the quaint allure of Moda. The cobblestone streets beneath your feet, the aroma of coffee lingering in the air, and the distant murmur of the Bosphorus—it's not just a location; it's an invitation to experience the bohemian heartbeat of Istanbul.

1. Bohemian Retreat: Moda's Timeless Appeal

Enter Moda, not just a neighborhood, but a bohemian retreat where creativity flourishes amidst the backdrop of historic charm. The vintage shops and art galleries lining the streets aren't just stores; they're portals into Moda's unique blend of nostalgia and contemporary flair.

Anecdote Alert: Moda isn't just a neighborhood; it has a literary legacy. Renowned Turkish writer Sait Faik Abasiyanik, captivated by Moda's charm, used to write about the district's streets and characters in his stories.

2. Simit on the Shore: A Seaside Tradition

Stroll along Moda's seaside promenade, not just a walk, but a leisurely journey with the Bosphorus as your companion. The simit vendors, selling the traditional Turkish sesame bread, aren't just street sellers; they're purveyors of a beloved seaside tradition.

Quirky Detail: Simit isn't just bread; it's a cultural icon. Enjoying a fresh simit by the Bosphorus isn't just a snack; it's a sensory experience that locals have cherished for generations.

3. Cafe Culture: Waterside Delights

Indulge in Moda's cafe culture, not just a coffee break, but a ritual of sipping Turkish tea or coffee while overlooking the Bosphorus. The waterfront cafes with colorful cushions and vintage decor aren't just places to drink; they're havens where time seems to slow down.

Fun Fact: Moda's cafes aren't just for refreshments; they have been meeting points for artists, poets, and thinkers, fostering a sense of community and inspiration.

4. Murals and Street Art: Moda's Creative Canvases

Admire Moda's murals and street art, not just graffiti, but vibrant expressions that adorn the neighborhood's walls. The artists behind these creations aren't just painters; they're contributors to Moda's evolving visual narrative.

Insider Insight: Moda's street art isn't just decorative; it often carries cultural and social messages, providing a unique perspective on the neighborhood's identity.

5. Moda's Timeless Cinema: Rexx Movie Theater

Visit the Rexx Movie Theater, not just a cinema, but a cultural landmark that has stood the test of time. The vintage marquee and red velvet seats aren't just elements of decor; they're echoes of cinematic history in Moda.

Anecdote Alert: Rexx Movie Theater isn't just a place to watch films; it has been a cultural hub since the early 20th century, witnessing the evolution of cinema and audience tastes.

6. Moda's Green Oasis: Moda Park

Relax in Moda Park, not just a park, but a green oasis where locals unwind amidst the shade of century-old trees. The fountains, benches, and flowerbeds aren't just park features; they're elements that enhance Moda's reputation as a peaceful retreat.

Fun Fact: Moda Park isn't just a recreational space; it hosts events, concerts, and festivals, bringing the community together in celebration.

Standing at the GPS coordinates of Moda District, you're not just in a location; you're in the heart of

Istanbul's bohemian haven. The coordinates mark the gateway to a neighborhood where creativity, nostalgia, and the gentle embrace of the Bosphorus converge. As you explore Moda, may you feel the echoes of its literary legacy, artistic spirit, and the timeless allure that has made it a cherished retreat on the Asian shores of Istanbul.

4.3.2 Haydarpasa - GPS Location: Where History Echoes Across the Bosphorus

Embark on a historical voyage as you follow the coordinates to Haydarpasa, a landmark that stands proudly on the Asian shores of the Bosphorus. Beyond being a train station, it's a symbol of Istanbul's rich railway heritage and a witness to the city's evolving narrative.

GPS Location: Haydarpasa

Latitude: 40.9926° N

Longitude: 29.0202° E

Picture this: You, standing at the coordinates, with Haydarpasa stretching before you like a time-travel portal. The rhythmic sound of departing trains, the grandeur of the architecture—it's not just a location; it's a gateway to Istanbul's railway history.

1. Architectural Majesty: Haydarpasa's Timeless Facade

Enter Haydarpasa, not just a train station, but an architectural masterpiece that blends the charm of Neo-Renaissance design with Ottoman motifs. The soaring clock tower and intricate details aren't just elements; they're echoes of a bygone era when railway travel was synonymous with elegance.

Anecdote Alert: Haydarpasa isn't just a station; it has been a setting for films, novels, and poems, becoming a cultural symbol that transcends its functional role.

2. A Railway Chronicle: Haydarpasa's Historical Significance

Explore the station's history, not just facts and figures, but a chronicle that spans over a century. The railway lines branching out from Haydarpasa aren't just tracks;

they're conduits of stories, connecting Istanbul to Anatolia and beyond.

Quirky Detail: Haydarpasa isn't just a terminal; it played a vital role during World War I, serving as a military hospital and witnessing historical events during the Ottoman era.

3. Seaside Panorama: Bosphorus Views from Haydarpasa

Gaze at the Bosphorus from Haydarpasa's waterfront, not just a view, but a panoramic spectacle that captures the essence of Istanbul's maritime allure. The passing ships and the minarets on the European side aren't just distant scenes; they're living tableaus framed by the station's grand arches.

Fun Fact: Haydarpasa's waterfront isn't just a place for scenic strolls; it has been a backdrop for countless photographers and artists seeking to capture Istanbul's unique juxtaposition of history and modernity.

4. Haydarpasa's Revival: Restoration Efforts

Learn about ongoing restoration efforts, not just construction projects, but endeavors to preserve Haydarpasa's architectural grandeur. The scaffolding and conservation teams aren't just signs of maintenance; they're guardians ensuring that this architectural gem stands proudly for future generations.

Insider Insight: The restoration of Haydarpasa isn't just about preserving a building; it's a commitment to safeguarding a piece of Istanbul's identity and cultural heritage.

5. Commuter Culture: Daily Life at Haydarpasa

Observe the daily hustle and bustle, not just a crowd, but a diverse tapestry of commuters, tourists, and locals. The vendors selling simit and tea aren't just sellers; they're part of the dynamic atmosphere that defines Haydarpasa's role as a transportation hub.

Anecdote Alert: Haydarpasa isn't just about arrivals and departures; it's a setting for reunions, farewells, and the ebb and flow of human stories unfolding against the backdrop of railway journeys.

6. Haydarpasa's Literary Echoes: Tales of Travel

Immerse yourself in the literary echoes of Haydarpasa, not just a station, but a muse that has inspired writers, poets, and storytellers. The books and novels set in or inspired by Haydarpasa aren't just literary works; they're invitations to embark on imaginative journeys through Istanbul's railway history.

Fun Fact: Haydarpasa isn't just a place in literature; it has been a setting for real-life love stories and chance encounters, adding a touch of romance to the station's narrative.

Standing at the GPS coordinates of Haydarpasa, you're not just at a location; you're at the intersection of history, culture, and the timeless allure of rail travel. The coordinates mark the gateway to a station that has witnessed the ebb and flow of Istanbul's narrative, from the Ottoman Empire to the present day. As you explore Haydarpasa, may you feel the echoes of bygone eras and the vibrant pulse of a station that remains a living testament to Istanbul's enduring spirit.

4.3.3 Kadikoy Market - GPS Location: Culinary Odyssey in the Heart of Kadikoy

Embark on a sensory journey through the bustling streets of Kadikoy Market, where the symphony of colors, aromas, and flavors converge to create a culinary haven on Istanbul's Asian side. Follow the coordinates to discover a market that transcends the ordinary, offering an immersive experience for both seasoned food enthusiasts and curious wanderers.

GPS Location: Kadikoy Market

Latitude: 40.9852° N

Longitude: 29.0279° E

Visualize this: You, standing at the coordinates, surrounded by the lively atmosphere of Kadikoy Market. The stalls brimming with fresh produce, the animated banter of vendors, and the tantalizing scents—it's not just a location; it's an invitation to savor the gastronomic delights of Istanbul.

1. Bazaar Ballet: Kadikoy's Culinary Stage

Enter Kadikoy Market, not just a marketplace, but a culinary stage where fresh ingredients take center stage in a mesmerizing ballet of flavors. The vibrant stalls and bustling aisles aren't just places to shop; they're a visual feast that unfolds against the backdrop of Kadikoy's lively spirit.

Anecdote Alert: Kadikoy Market isn't just about commerce; it has been a setting for local gatherings, celebrations, and the vibrant tapestry of everyday life in this Anatolian enclave.

2. Fresh Bounty: Local Produce Extravaganza

Explore the array of fresh produce, not just fruits and vegetables, but a cornucopia of colors that reflect the diversity of Anatolian agriculture. The farmers and vendors aren't just sellers; they're storytellers, sharing the tales behind each plump tomato, aromatic herb, and crisp cucumber.

Quirky Detail: Kadikoy Market isn't just about selling; it's a communal space where locals often share recipes, cooking tips, and the joys of seasonal produce.

3. Aroma Alcove: Spices and Delicacies

Wander through the spice stalls, not just vendors, but spice maestros who offer an olfactory journey through the fragrant treasures of Turkish cuisine. The saffron, sumac, and cumin aren't just spices; they're aromatic time capsules that transport you to the heart of Anatolian culinary traditions.

Fun Fact: Kadikoy's spice stalls aren't just places to buy; they often reflect the neighborhood's multicultural influences, offering spices from various regions of Turkey and beyond.

4. Delightful Detour: Sweet Stops and Turkish Delight

Indulge your sweet tooth at the dessert stands, not just confections, but a parade of Turkish delight, baklava, and other delectable treats. The vendors offering sweet delights aren't just merchants; they're confectionery artisans, each treat a testament to the rich heritage of Turkish sweets.

Insider Insight: Kadikoy's dessert stalls aren't just places to satisfy cravings; they are gateways to understanding the intricate artistry and cultural significance behind each sweet creation.

5. Seafood Spectacle: Fresh Catches by the Bosphorus

Visit the seafood section, not just a market segment, but a spectacle of the day's catch displayed in a dazzling array. The fishmongers aren't just vendors; they're keepers of a maritime tradition, providing a glimpse into the culinary treasures sourced from the Bosphorus.

Anecdote Alert: Kadikoy Market's seafood section isn't just about commerce; it has been a subject of inspiration for artists and photographers capturing the visual poetry of fresh seafood.

6. Gastronomic Conversations: Street Food Delights

Relish the street food stalls, not just eateries, but venues where gastronomic conversations unfold amidst the sizzle and aroma of kebabs, simit, and other savory delights. The street food vendors aren't just cooks; they're culinary storytellers, infusing each dish with the spirit of Kadikoy's street food culture.

Fun Fact: Kadikoy's street food stalls aren't just for quick bites; they often become communal spaces where locals and visitors bond over shared meals and the joy of discovery.

Standing at the GPS coordinates of Kadikoy Market, you're not just in a location; you're at the heart of Istanbul's culinary soul. The coordinates mark the gateway to a market where every ingredient, every aroma, and every vendor tells a story of Anatolian flavors. As you explore Kadikoy Market, may your senses be delighted, your palate satisfied, and your journey through Istanbul's gastronomic wonders become a savory memory etched into the fabric of your travel tale.

5

THEMED ITINERARIES

5.1 Culinary Delights: A Feast for the Senses in Istanbul

Prepare for a gastronomic odyssey as you explore the culinary wonders of Istanbul. From savory kebabs that melt in your mouth to sweet delicacies that dance on your palate, the city's food scene is a celebration of flavors that transcends mere sustenance. Follow your taste buds and let the symphony of spices, textures, and aromas guide you through Istanbul's culinary tapestry.

Imagine this: You, seated at a bustling eatery, surrounded by the intoxicating scent of grilling meat, the lively chatter of locals, and the promise of a culinary adventure unfolding before you. It's not just a meal; it's an immersion into Istanbul's rich and diverse food culture.

1. Kebab Kingdom: Savory Perfection

Embark on a kebab pilgrimage, not just a meal, but a journey through the many incarnations of this Turkish culinary icon. From the succulent Adana kebabs to the mouthwatering doner, each bite tells a story of centuries-old traditions and the mastery of Anatolian flavors.

Anecdote Alert: Did you know that the doner kebab, a beloved street food worldwide, originated in Bursa, Turkey, in the 19th century? Its popularity soared, becoming a symbol of Turkish gastronomy.

2. Meze Magic: Small Plates, Big Flavors

Delight in the world of mezes, not just appetizers, but an assortment of small plates that invite you to savor a multitude of flavors. The hummus, stuffed grape leaves, and yogurt-based dishes aren't just starters; they're an introduction to the art of communal dining and shared pleasures.

Quirky Detail: In Turkish culture, mezes are often enjoyed with rakı, an anise-flavored spirit. The combination of meze and rakı is not just a culinary pairing; it's a social ritual known as "meze sofrası," meaning "meze table."

3. Street Food Symphony: Simit, Balik Ekmek, and More

Immerse yourself in Istanbul's vibrant street food scene, not just quick bites, but a symphony of flavors that unfold as you stroll through bustling neighborhoods. Simit, a sesame-crusted bread ring, and balik ekmek, a fish sandwich, aren't just snacks; they're portable delights that capture the essence of Istanbul's culinary spirit.

Fun Fact: The simit isn't just a popular street food; it has deep historical roots. It was introduced to the Ottoman Empire by a Jewish baker from Thessaloniki in the 16th century.

4. Sweet Temptations: Baklava, Turkish Delight, and More

Indulge your sweet tooth in Istanbul's array of desserts, not just confections, but heavenly treats that range from the flaky layers of baklava to the delicate delights of Turkish delight. Each bite is a celebration of the city's love affair with sugar and the mastery of artisanal confectionery.

Insider Insight: Baklava isn't just a dessert; it's an art form. The intricate layering of phyllo dough and nuts, soaked in syrup, is a labor of love that requires skill and precision.

5. Turkish Tea Time: Sip and Savor

Experience the art of Turkish tea, not just a beverage, but a cultural institution that accompanies moments of reflection and socializing. The small tulip-shaped glasses aren't just vessels; they're a symbol of hospitality, offering warmth and connection in every sip.

Anecdote Alert: Turkish tea is not just about the drink; it's about the ritual. It's common for locals to engage in deep conversations and share laughter over a cup of tea in traditional tea houses or at home.

6. Culinary Crossroads: Bazaars and Markets

Explore the bazaars and markets, not just shopping destinations, but treasure troves of culinary delights waiting to be discovered. The spice-scented air, the vibrant displays of produce, and the lively banter of vendors aren't just market scenes; they're immersive experiences that connect you to the heart of Istanbul's food culture.

Fun Fact: Istanbul's Grand Bazaar isn't just a historic market; it's one of the world's oldest and largest covered markets, with over 4,000 shops spanning 61 streets.

Dive into the culinary delights of Istanbul, where each dish is a brushstroke on the canvas of the city's rich history and cultural tapestry. As you savor the flavors, may you not just eat, but partake in a gastronomic adventure that leaves an indelible mark on your Istanbul experience—a tapestry woven with the threads of centuries-old recipes, cultural influences, and the warmth of Turkish hospitality.

5.2 Cultural Immersion: Unveiling Istanbul's Kaleidoscope of Traditions

Step beyond the surface and immerse yourself in Istanbul's vibrant cultural tapestry. From ancient rituals to modern expressions, the city's cultural landscape is a kaleidoscope of traditions waiting to be discovered. Traverse the historic streets, engage with locals, and let the city reveal its soul through captivating stories, lively performances, and immersive experiences.

Envision this: You, navigating the labyrinthine alleys, the call to prayer echoing in the distance, vibrant colors of traditional costumes, and the palpable energy of a city deeply rooted in its cultural heritage. It's not just a journey; it's an invitation to become a part of Istanbul's living narrative.

1. Call to Prayer: Echoes of Faith and Harmony

Experience the call to prayer, not just a religious practice, but a melodious reverie that resonates across Istanbul's minarets. The hauntingly beautiful tunes aren't just sounds; they're a reminder of the city's rich Islamic heritage and the unity found in the act of worship.

Anecdote Alert: Did you know that the call to prayer, or adhan, has been echoing across Istanbul since the 15th century? It's not just a religious proclamation; it's an integral part of the city's soundscape.

2. Traditional Turkish Baths: A Ritual of Renewal

Indulge in the age-old tradition of Turkish baths, not just a spa experience, but a ritual that dates back to the Ottoman era. The marble hammams, scented with fragrant oils, aren't just bathing spaces; they're sanctuaries where cleansing takes on a cultural significance.

Quirky Detail: The Turkish bath isn't just about cleanliness; it's a social activity. In the past, people of all ages and social classes would gather in hammams, creating a communal space for relaxation and conversation.

3. Whirling Dervishes: Mystical Dance of Sufism

Witness the mesmerizing dance of the Whirling Dervishes, not just a performance, but a spiritual practice that transcends the boundaries of the physical world. The swirling white robes and meditative movements aren't just a spectacle; they're an expression of Sufi philosophy and devotion.

Fun Fact: The Whirling Dervishes aren't just performers; they are members of the Mevlevi Order, founded in the

13th century. The dance, called Sema, symbolizes the soul's journey toward spiritual truth.

4. Coffeehouse Conversations: The Art of Turkish Coffee

Engage in coffeehouse culture, not just a caffeine fix, but a tradition deeply ingrained in Turkish social life. The aromatic Turkish coffee isn't just a beverage; it's a symbol of hospitality, a medium for fortune-telling, and a catalyst for intimate conversations.

Insider Insight: Turkish coffee isn't just about the coffee itself; it's about the brewing process, the serving rituals, and the meaningful conversations that unfold over a cup.

5. Carpet Weaving: Threads of Heritage

Explore the art of carpet weaving, not just craftsmanship, but a centuries-old tradition that weaves stories, symbols, and cultural heritage into every intricate pattern. The vibrant colors and meticulous designs aren't just floor coverings; they're expressions of Anatolian artistry.

Anecdote Alert: Turkish carpets aren't just textiles; they are often considered works of art. The weaving process is a labor-intensive craft passed down through generations.

6. Street Performers: Art in Unexpected Places

Encounter street performers, not just entertainers, but artists who transform public spaces into stages for their talents. The musicians, painters, and performers aren't just passersby; they're contributors to Istanbul's dynamic street culture, adding artistic flair to unexpected corners.

Fun Fact: Istanbul's street performers aren't just individuals showcasing their talents; they often become part of the city's narrative, leaving a lasting impression on both locals and visitors.

Dive into the cultural immersion of Istanbul, where every step unveils a new facet of the city's rich heritage. As you engage with rituals, witness traditional arts, and become part of the vibrant street life, may you not just observe but become a participant in the living story of Istanbul—a city where history, tradition, and contemporary expressions harmoniously converge.

5.3 Historical Marvels: Traversing the Epochs in Istanbul

Embark on a journey through time as you explore Istanbul's historical marvels—testaments to the city's rich past that unfold like chapters in a captivating story. From ancient structures to imperial palaces, each site bears witness to the ebb and flow of empires, creating a living museum within the city. Let the stones beneath your feet whisper tales of Byzantine emperors, Ottoman sultans, and the resilience of a city that has stood the test of time.

Envision this: You, standing amidst towering structures, the echoes of ancient footsteps reverberating, and the grandeur of historical wonders surrounding you. It's not just a visit; it's a pilgrimage through the epochs, where every stone has a story to tell.

1. Hagia Sophia: A Divine Metamorphosis

Step into the Hagia Sophia, not just a building, but a living chronicle of architectural evolution. The massive dome, intricate mosaics, and the interplay of light aren't just elements; they're reflections of a structure that has witnessed the Byzantine Empire, the Ottoman conquest, and the modern Turkish Republic.

Anecdote Alert: Did you know that Hagia Sophia was originally built as a cathedral in the 6th century, later converted into a mosque, and finally into a museum? Its diverse history isn't just a narrative; it's a reflection of Istanbul's cultural complexity.

2. Topkapi Palace: Imperial Splendor Unveiled

Wander through the halls of Topkapi Palace, not just a residence, but a sprawling complex that once housed Ottoman sultans and their courts. The opulent chambers, stunning gardens, and the Harem aren't just rooms; they're portals into the lavish lifestyle of the Ottoman Empire.

Quirky Detail: The Imperial Harem wasn't just a secluded space for the sultan's family; it was a power center where influential women played significant roles in shaping the empire's destiny.

3. Blue Mosque: A Symphony in Blue and Gold

Enter the Blue Mosque, not just a place of worship, but an architectural masterpiece adorned with intricate tiles and cascading domes. The rhythmic patterns, towering minarets, and the expansive courtyard aren't just features; they're a reflection of Ottoman grandeur and the artistic prowess of the era.

Fun Fact: The Blue Mosque, officially known as the Sultan Ahmed Mosque, wasn't just a place for prayers; it was designed to rival the Hagia Sophia in grandeur, showcasing the Ottoman Empire's architectural prowess.

4. Basilica Cistern: Subterranean Splendor

Descend into the Basilica Cistern, not just an underground reservoir, but a mysterious chamber adorned with colossal Medusa heads and intricately carved columns. The dimly lit pathways, the reflective waters, and the eerie silence aren't just elements; they're glimpses into a hidden world beneath the city's surface.

Insider Insight: The Basilica Cistern wasn't just a utilitarian structure; it was a crucial component of

Byzantine Constantinople's water supply system, showcasing the city's advanced engineering.

5. Grand Bazaar: Commerce Through the Ages

Navigate the labyrinthine alleys of the Grand Bazaar, not just a market, but a historic marketplace that has been a hub of commerce for centuries. The vibrant stalls, the eclectic array of goods, and the animated haggling aren't just transactions; they're echoes of a trade tradition that has shaped Istanbul's identity.

Anecdote Alert: The Grand Bazaar wasn't just a place for buying and selling; it became a microcosm of the city itself, with its own streets, mosques, and even a police force.

6. Suleymaniye Mosque: Architectural Majesty

Marvel at the Suleymaniye Mosque, not just a place of worship, but an architectural marvel that crowns the city's skyline. The sweeping courtyards, majestic domes, and the panoramic views of Istanbul aren't just scenic; they're a testament to the imperial vision of Suleiman the Magnificent.

Fun Fact: Suleymaniye Mosque wasn't just a spiritual center; it housed a complex with schools, a hospital, and even a kitchen that provided meals for the needy, embodying the Ottoman commitment to social welfare.

As you traverse the historical marvels of Istanbul, may each step be a connection to the city's storied past. These landmarks aren't just monuments; they are living witnesses to the rise and fall of empires, the interweaving of cultures, and the resilience of a city that continues to stand as a testament to the enduring spirit of Istanbul.

5.4 Outdoor Adventures: Embracing Nature's Playground in Istanbul

Escape the urban hustle and immerse yourself in Istanbul's natural wonders, where lush greenery, panoramic views, and outdoor pursuits await. From serene parks to breathtaking viewpoints, the city offers a diverse range of outdoor adventures that allow you to connect with nature while savoring the beauty of Istanbul's landscape. Lace up your walking shoes, breathe in the fresh air, and let the outdoors become your playground.

Picture this: You, traversing scenic trails, the gentle rustle of leaves overhead, and the cityscape unfolding before you. It's not just an adventure; it's a rejuvenating journey through Istanbul's green oases, where every step is an invitation to discover the city's natural allure.

1. Belgrade Forest: Serenity in the City's Embrace

Explore the Belgrade Forest, not just a wooded area, but a vast expanse that provides a peaceful retreat from the urban buzz. The towering trees, meandering paths, and the crisp forest air aren't just elements; they're an invitation to escape into nature without leaving the city.

Anecdote Alert: Belgrade Forest wasn't just a recreational space; it played a crucial role during the Ottoman Empire, serving as a hunting ground for the sultans.

2. Bosphorus Cruise: A Nautical Tapestry

Embark on a Bosphorus cruise, not just a boat ride, but a nautical journey that unveils Istanbul's iconic skyline from a unique perspective. The shimmering waters, historic landmarks, and the gentle sway of the boat aren't just maritime experiences; they're moments of tranquility on the Bosphorus strait.

Quirky Detail: Bosphorus cruises aren't just daytime excursions; evening cruises offer a magical view of Istanbul's illuminated skyline, creating a romantic ambiance.

3. Camlica Hill: Panoramic Splendor

Ascend to Camlica Hill, not just an elevated point, but the highest peak in Istanbul that provides panoramic views of the city below. The sprawling landscapes, the distant minarets, and the vast sky aren't just sights; they're a visual feast that captures Istanbul's expansive beauty.

Fun Fact: Camlica Hill wasn't just a natural landmark; it became a symbol of urban planning in Istanbul, offering a green sanctuary for locals and visitors alike.

4. Prince Islands: Tranquil Escapes

Sail to the Prince Islands, not just a cluster of isles, but a tranquil escape where horse-drawn carriages replace cars and the sea breeze carries the scent of pine. The Victorian-era mansions, the serene beaches, and the unhurried pace aren't just features; they're a step back in time to a bygone era.

Insider Insight: The Prince Islands weren't just a summer retreat; they served as places of exile for Byzantine princes and other notable figures throughout history.

5. Emirgan Park: Blooms and Beyond

Stroll through Emirgan Park, not just a green space, but a botanical haven where seasonal blooms paint the landscape in a riot of colors. The vibrant tulip gardens, the meandering pathways, and the serene ponds aren't just park features; they're a celebration of Istanbul's horticultural beauty.

Anecdote Alert: Emirgan Park wasn't just a public space; it hosted the annual Istanbul Tulip Festival, showcasing thousands of tulip varieties and attracting visitors from around the world.

6. Yoros Castle: Coastal Ruins

Hike to Yoros Castle, not just ancient ruins, but a coastal fortress that overlooks the meeting point of the Black Sea and the Bosphorus. The rugged trails, the weathered stone walls, and the expansive sea views aren't just archaeological remnants; they're a glimpse into Istanbul's maritime history.

Fun Fact: Yoros Castle wasn't just a military stronghold; it played a strategic role during various periods, from the Byzantine Empire to the Ottoman era.

Embarking on outdoor adventures in Istanbul isn't just about exploring nature; it's a chance to discover hidden gems, experience the city's diverse landscapes, and create memories amidst the embrace of the great outdoors. May your outdoor pursuits be filled with awe, relaxation, and the joy of connecting with Istanbul's natural wonders.

6

SUSTAINABLE TRAVEL TIPS

6.1 Eco-Friendly Accommodations: Where Sustainability Meets Serenity

In Istanbul, a new wave of accommodation options is emerging—places where the commitment to sustainability harmonizes with the charm of hospitality. These eco-friendly havens not only provide a comfortable stay but also weave a narrative of environmental responsibility into the tapestry of your travel experience. Step into a world where conscientious living meets luxurious comfort.

Envision this: You, arriving at a tranquil eco-friendly retreat, the architecture blending seamlessly with nature, and the air carrying a sense of responsibility for the environment. It's not just a place to rest; it's a sanctuary where sustainability and serenity converge.

1. Green Roofs and Verdant Walls: Harmony with Nature

Enter accommodations adorned with green roofs and verdant walls, not just architectural features, but living canvases that contribute to energy efficiency and create a haven for local flora. The gentle rustle of leaves overhead and the vibrant colors of nature aren't just aesthetics; they're the embodiment of a commitment to eco-conscious living.

Anecdote Alert: Some eco-friendly accommodations in Istanbul go beyond conventional landscaping, integrating local plant species that contribute to the preservation of indigenous biodiversity.

2. Solar Elegance: Harnessing the Power of the Sun

Stay in establishments where solar panels aren't just fixtures on the rooftop; they are silent champions harnessing the power of the sun to generate energy. The warm glow of solar-powered lights and the subtle hum of sustainable energy aren't just utilities; they're testaments to reducing carbon footprints in the heart of the city.

Quirky Detail: A few eco-conscious hotels in Istanbul have adopted innovative solar-powered charging stations, allowing guests to recharge their devices using clean energy.

3. Waste Warriors: Recycling and Upcycling

Experience accommodations that have embraced a zero-waste philosophy, not just a practice, but a commitment to recycling and upcycling that extends from the kitchen to the guest rooms. The quirky charm of upcycled furniture and the diligent sorting of recyclables aren't just eco-friendly practices; they're small gestures making a big impact.

Fun Fact: Some eco-friendly hotels in Istanbul collaborate with local artisans to transform discarded materials into unique, aesthetically pleasing décor, adding a touch of sustainability to your surroundings.

4. Locally Sourced Amenities: Supporting Community

Indulge in amenities sourced locally, not just toiletries, but products that support local businesses and reduce the ecological footprint. The aromatic allure of locally crafted soaps and the eco-friendly packaging aren't just indulgences; they're a connection to the vibrant community surrounding your accommodation.

Insider Insight: Eco-conscious hotels often partner with local artisans and producers, creating a unique guest experience while contributing to the sustainability of Istanbul's local economy.

5. Water Wisdom: Conservation in Every Drop

Stay in accommodations that prioritize water conservation, not just through low-flow faucets and efficient irrigation systems, but through awareness campaigns that educate guests about responsible water usage. The soothing sound of a rainwater harvesting system and the awareness of minimizing water waste aren't just eco-friendly initiatives; they're invitations to be mindful stewards of precious resources.

Anecdote Alert: Some eco-friendly lodgings in Istanbul share fascinating facts about the city's historical water management systems, showcasing how ancient civilizations ingeniously conserved water.

6. Cultural Conservation: Preserving Heritage

Choose accommodations committed to preserving cultural heritage, not just through architectural restoration but by engaging in community initiatives that promote responsible tourism. The blend of historic charm and modern eco-conscious practices isn't just a juxtaposition; it's a celebration of the past and a vision for a sustainable future.

Fun Fact: A few eco-friendly accommodations in Istanbul are located in meticulously restored historic buildings, offering guests a chance to experience the city's rich cultural heritage while supporting preservation efforts.

As you check into these eco-friendly retreats in Istanbul, you're not just booking a room; you're participating in a movement towards responsible travel. These accommodations aren't just places to stay; they are gateways to a more sustainable and mindful exploration of Istanbul—a city where your presence leaves a positive impact on the environment and supports the local community.

6.2 Responsible Dining Choices: Savoring Sustainability in Every Bite

Istanbul's culinary scene extends beyond delicious flavors; it's a journey into responsible dining where every meal becomes an opportunity to support sustainable practices and local communities. From farm-to-table delights to eco-conscious establishments, explore dining choices that not only tantalize your taste buds but also leave a positive imprint on the environment.

Visualize this: You, seated at a table adorned with locally sourced produce, the aroma of freshly prepared dishes wafting through the air, and the knowledge that your culinary adventure is a celebration of sustainability. It's not just a meal; it's a conscious choice that flavors every bite with responsibility.

1. Farm-to-Table Feasts: A Culinary Connection to the Land

Indulge in farm-to-table dining experiences, not just meals, but culinary journeys that bring the freshness of local farms to your plate. The vibrant colors of freshly harvested vegetables and the rich aroma of locally sourced meats aren't just ingredients; they're a testament to supporting local agriculture and reducing the carbon footprint of your dining experience.

Anecdote Alert: Some Istanbul restaurants cultivate their own rooftop gardens, ensuring a direct and sustainable supply of herbs and vegetables, creating a literal farm-to-table experience.

2. Seafood Sustainability: Oceans on Your Plate

Opt for seafood establishments committed to sustainable fishing practices, not just delectable dishes, but a responsible approach that safeguards marine ecosystems. The ocean-fresh flavors and the knowledge that your meal supports responsible fishing practices aren't just culinary delights; they're contributions to the health of our oceans.

Quirky Detail: Istanbul's seafood restaurants often collaborate with local fishermen who adhere to sustainable fishing methods, ensuring the long-term well-being of marine life.

3. Locavore Delights: Celebrating Local Flavors

Embark on a journey of locavore dining, not just a meal, but an exploration of Istanbul's diverse culinary landscape where local ingredients take center stage. The robust flavors of artisanal cheeses, the aromatic spices from nearby markets, and the innovative twists on traditional recipes aren't just culinary choices; they're a celebration of the rich tapestry of Istanbul's food culture.

Fun Fact: Some Istanbul chefs actively engage with local farmers and producers, collaborating to create exclusive dishes that showcase the unique flavors of the region.

4. Zero-Waste Gastronomy: Culinary Consciousness

Delight in zero-waste gastronomy, not just a dining experience, but a commitment to minimizing food waste and environmental impact. The creative use of food scraps, the emphasis on portion control, and the eco-friendly packaging aren't just culinary practices; they're a movement towards responsible consumption that transcends the boundaries of the kitchen.

Insider Insight: A few Istanbul restaurants are pioneering innovative approaches to zero-waste gastronomy, transforming surplus food into delicious meals for local communities in need.

5. Eco-Conscious Cafés: Brewing Sustainability

Choose eco-conscious cafés, not just for a caffeine fix, but for the mindful sourcing of coffee beans and eco-friendly practices that extend from bean to cup. The rich aroma of ethically sourced coffee and the knowledge that your coffee break supports fair trade practices aren't just moments of indulgence; they're small gestures that contribute to a global movement for ethical coffee consumption.

Anecdote Alert: Some Istanbul cafés collaborate directly with coffee farmers, ensuring fair wages and ethical treatment throughout the coffee production chain.

6. Cultural Culinary Preservation: Time-Honored Techniques

Dine in establishments committed to preserving cultural culinary traditions, not just for exquisite flavors, but as custodians of recipes passed down through generations. The handcrafted dishes, the dedication to preserving traditional cooking methods, and the culinary stories shared by the chefs aren't just meals; they're tributes to the cultural heritage of Istanbul's gastronomy.

Fun Fact: Istanbul's culinary scene is dotted with eateries where chefs take pride in reviving ancient recipes, ensuring that the city's culinary traditions continue to thrive.

As you navigate Istanbul's dining scene, savoring every bite becomes a journey into responsible and conscious choices. These culinary establishments aren't just places to eat; they are ambassadors of sustainability, preserving local flavors, supporting ethical practices, and offering a delicious way to engage with Istanbul's commitment to a greener and more responsible future.

6.3 Public Transportation Initiatives: Navigating Istanbul Sustainably

In a city where the past and present seamlessly coexist, Istanbul's public transportation initiatives are propelling it into a sustainable future. From the nostalgic charm of ferries to the efficiency of modern metro systems, embrace the city's commitment to eco-friendly commuting. Step aboard the vessels of progress and embark on a journey where each mode of transportation is not just a means to an end but a part of Istanbul's sustainable tapestry.

Picture this: You, gliding across the Bosphorus on a ferry, the rhythmic hum of a tram beneath you, and the seamless transition between ancient and modern modes of transport. It's not just a commute; it's a ride through Istanbul's commitment to a greener, more accessible tomorrow.

1. Nostalgic Ferries: A Voyage Across Time

Embark on Istanbul's iconic ferries, not just vessels, but floating time machines that transport you across the city's historical and modern landscapes. The gentle sway of the boat, the panoramic views of the skyline, and the harmonious blend of tradition and technology aren't just a journey; they're a celebration of Istanbul's maritime legacy.

Anecdote Alert: Istanbul's ferries aren't just a mode of transportation; they've become symbols of the city, immortalized in literature, art, and the memories of both locals and visitors.

2. Tram Rides through History: Navigating Nostalgia

Board the city's trams, not just vehicles, but moving narratives that traverse historic routes and bring the past to life. The rhythmic clatter of the tram wheels, the cobblestone streets passing beneath you, and the architectural wonders unfolding outside the window aren't just a commute; they're a poetic journey through the heart of Istanbul's cultural heritage.

Quirky Detail: Istanbul's nostalgic trams aren't just a nod to the past; they are meticulously maintained vintage vehicles, adding a touch of charm to the city's bustling streets.

3. Metro Marvels: Subterranean Efficiency

Descend into Istanbul's modern metro system, not just tunnels, but subterranean arteries that efficiently connect the city's diverse neighborhoods. The futuristic hum of the metro, the speed and precision of the trains, and the seamless integration of technology and sustainability aren't just a commute; they're a testament to Istanbul's commitment to modern urban living.

Fun Fact: Istanbul's metro system isn't just a recent development; the city's first underground railway, the Tünel, was inaugurated in 1875, making it one of the oldest subways in the world.

4. Bus Networks: Wheels of Connectivity

Explore Istanbul's comprehensive bus network, not just vehicles, but interconnected arteries that span the city's vast expanse. The rhythmic hum of the engine, the vibrant mosaic of passengers, and the network's adaptability to Istanbul's dynamic urban landscape aren't just a ride; they're a journey through the veins of a city that pulsates with life.

Insider Insight: Istanbul's bus network isn't just about getting from point A to B; it's a cultural experience, where the diverse demographics of the city converge in a shared space.

5. Bicycle-Friendly Initiatives: Pedaling Progress

Embrace Istanbul's bicycle-friendly initiatives, not just lanes, but pathways that invite you to pedal through the city's historic streets and along the scenic shores. The gentle whirr of bicycle wheels, the breeze on your face, and the sense of freedom aren't just a ride; they're a contribution to Istanbul's green initiatives and a healthy, sustainable lifestyle.

Anecdote Alert: Istanbul's bicycle culture isn't just a recent phenomenon; it has roots in the 19th century, when cycling clubs flourished, transforming the city's streets.

6. Water Taxis: Aquatic Commutes

Embark on Istanbul's water taxis, not just boats, but aquatic shuttles that navigate the city's waterways, providing a unique and efficient mode of transport. The gentle lapping of waves against the hull, the panoramic views of the cityscape, and the sense of tranquility on the water aren't just a commute; they're a reminder of Istanbul's maritime legacy.

Fun Fact: Istanbul's water taxis aren't just for locals; they are a favorite mode of transport for savvy visitors, offering a picturesque and efficient way to explore the city.

As you traverse Istanbul's public transportation network, each mode of transport becomes a chapter in the city's story—a tale of innovation, preservation, and progress. These initiatives aren't just about moving from one place to another; they are the threads weaving together the diverse fabric of Istanbul's neighborhoods, cultures, and histories.

6.4 Community Engagement Opportunities: Embrace Istanbul's Heartbeat

In Istanbul, community engagement isn't just an activity; it's a vibrant tapestry woven by the collective spirit of its residents. Dive into the city's heartbeat, where locals open their arms and share the richness of their culture, traditions, and stories. From volunteering initiatives to immersive experiences, discover opportunities that allow you to become not just a visitor but a valued member of Istanbul's dynamic community.

Imagine this: You, standing side by side with locals, hands shaping clay in a workshop, the laughter of children echoing in a community project, and the feeling of belonging as you contribute to the city's collective narrative. It's not just engagement; it's a dance with

Istanbul's essence, where every step leaves an imprint on the mosaic of community life.

1. Volunteer Ventures: Giving Back with Heart

Engage in volunteer projects, not just tasks, but opportunities to make a positive impact in the lives of Istanbul's residents. Whether you're teaching language skills, participating in community clean-ups, or contributing to local development projects, the sense of fulfillment and connection aren't just moments; they're threads weaving you into the fabric of Istanbul's social tapestry.

Anecdote Alert: Istanbul's volunteer initiatives aren't just about charity; they often lead to lasting friendships, creating bonds that transcend geographical boundaries.

2. Cultural Workshops: Handcrafting Memories

Participate in cultural workshops, not just activities, but hands-on experiences that immerse you in the traditional arts and crafts of Istanbul. From tile painting to calligraphy, the vibrant colors, and the rhythmic strokes of your creations aren't just crafts; they're personal expressions that become part of the city's cultural heritage.

Quirky Detail: Istanbul's artisans aren't just teachers; they are storytellers, sharing the narratives behind each craft and connecting you to the centuries-old traditions of the city.

3. Neighborhood Festivals: Celebrations of Unity

Attend neighborhood festivals, not just events, but lively celebrations that bring locals together in a riot of colors, music, and flavors. The joyful sounds of music, the tantalizing aromas of street food, and the communal spirit aren't just festivities; they're windows into the diverse identities that define Istanbul's neighborhoods.

Fun Fact: Istanbul's neighborhood festivals aren't just about entertainment; they often feature initiatives promoting sustainability, cultural exchange, and community well-being.

4. Community Gardens: Green Oases in the Urban Jungle

Join community garden projects, not just green spaces, but thriving oases where residents cultivate not just plants but a sense of community. The fragrance of blooming flowers, the shared joy of harvest, and the knowledge that you're contributing to Istanbul's green initiatives aren't just gardening activities; they're acts of stewardship for the city's environment.

Insider Insight: Istanbul's community gardens aren't just about horticulture; they are platforms for exchanging gardening wisdom, cultural practices, and fostering a sense of shared responsibility.

5. Storytelling Sessions: Narratives that Bind

Participate in storytelling sessions, not just narratives, but shared moments where locals regale you with tales of their lives, traditions, and the city's history. The animated gestures, the laughter, and the personal anecdotes aren't just stories; they're bridges connecting you to the human stories that shape Istanbul's identity.

Anecdote Alert: Istanbul's storytellers aren't just historians; they are living archives, offering a firsthand account of the city's evolution and the resilience of its people.

6. Language Exchange Gatherings: Connecting Through Words

Join language exchange gatherings, not just linguistic endeavors, but vibrant meetings where locals and visitors bridge cultural gaps through the exchange of language and ideas. The melodic flow of words, the shared laughter over language nuances, and the connections forged aren't just language sessions; they're pathways to understanding Istanbul's cultural diversity.

Fun Fact: Istanbul's language exchange events aren't just about mastering words; they often lead to cultural exchanges, fostering friendships that span the globe.

Engaging with Istanbul's community isn't just an option; it's an invitation to become part of a living, breathing narrative. Each interaction, whether volunteering, crafting, celebrating, or sharing stories, contributes to the intricate mosaic that makes Istanbul a city of warmth, diversity, and shared experiences. As you immerse yourself in these engagement opportunities, you're not just visiting Istanbul; you're becoming a cherished part of its dynamic and welcoming community.

7
LOCAL EVENTS CALENDAR

7.1 Festivals and Celebrations: Revelry in the Heart of Istanbul

In Istanbul, the calendar isn't just a collection of dates; it's a vibrant tapestry woven with festivals and celebrations that breathe life into the city's streets. Dive into the kaleidoscope of colors, music, and cultural revelry as Istanbul opens its arms to residents and visitors alike. From ancient traditions to contemporary festivities, discover the rhythm of the city through its captivating festivals.

Picture this: You, swept up in a sea of vibrant colors, the echoes of lively music filling the air, and the scent of delicious street food tempting your taste buds. It's not just an event; it's an immersion into the pulsating heart of Istanbul's cultural exuberance, where every celebration is a chapter in the city's rich narrative.

1. Istanbul International Film Festival: Cinematic Odyssey

Embark on a cinematic odyssey at the Istanbul International Film Festival, not just a movie marathon, but an exploration of diverse cultures, perspectives, and storytelling brilliance. The red carpet glamour, the anticipation in the air, and the shared love for the art of filmmaking aren't just screenings; they're a celebration of Istanbul's thriving film culture.

Quirky Detail: The Istanbul International Film Festival isn't just about Hollywood blockbusters; it showcases a rich selection of Turkish and international films, making it a cinephile's dream.

2. Istanbul Music Festival: Symphony under the Stars

Surrender to the enchanting melodies at the Istanbul Music Festival, not just concerts, but a symphony that echoes through historic venues, parks, and open-air spaces. The harmonious notes, the starlit ambiance, and the sense of being transported into a world of musical enchantment aren't just performances; they're a celebration of Istanbul's cultural legacy.

Anecdote Alert: The Istanbul Music Festival isn't just a modern affair; it traces its roots back to 1973, making it one of the oldest festivals of its kind in Turkey.

3. Istanbul Biennial: Art Unbound

Immerse yourself in a world where art knows no boundaries at the Istanbul Biennial, not just exhibitions, but a dynamic showcase of contemporary artistic expressions that push the limits. The avant-garde installations, the thought-provoking exhibits, and the vibrant conversations around modern art aren't just displays; they're a testament to Istanbul's position as a global art hub.

Fun Fact: The Istanbul Biennial isn't just confined to traditional gallery spaces; it often spills into unconventional venues, transforming the city itself into a canvas for artistic exploration.

4. Ramadan: Spiritual Reflection and Culinary Delights

Experience the holy month of Ramadan, not just fasting, but a time of spiritual reflection, community bonding, and delectable culinary traditions. The bustling energy of iftar gatherings, the fragrant aromas of traditional dishes, and the unity felt during shared meals aren't just religious practices; they're a cultural spectacle that showcases Istanbul's rich tapestry of traditions.

Insider Insight: During Ramadan, Istanbul's historic districts transform into vibrant hubs, with streets adorned with colorful lights, creating a magical ambiance for nightly celebrations.

5. Istanbul Jazz Festival: Rhythmic Revelry

Get into the groove at the Istanbul Jazz Festival, not just performances, but a rhythmic journey through genres, from traditional jazz to innovative fusions. The soulful melodies, the electric atmosphere, and the improvisational brilliance on stage aren't just concerts; they're a celebration of Istanbul's love affair with jazz.

Anecdote Alert: The Istanbul Jazz Festival isn't just about international headliners; it often features collaborations with local musicians, creating a harmonious blend of global and local sounds.

6. Istanbul Tulip Festival: Blooms Across the City

Witness the city burst into a riot of colors during the Istanbul Tulip Festival, not just flowers in bloom, but a spectacular display that blankets parks, gardens, and public spaces. The vibrant hues, the meticulous tulip arrangements, and the contagious enthusiasm for spring aren't just floral showcases; they're a celebration of renewal and the city's horticultural beauty.

Fun Fact: The Istanbul Tulip Festival isn't just a recent tradition; it draws inspiration from the Ottoman era, where tulips held significant cultural and symbolic importance.

As you navigate Istanbul's festival calendar, each celebration isn't just an event; it's a dynamic expression of the city's soul. From the red carpets to the blooming tulips, the jazz-infused nights to the spiritual reflections of Ramadan, Istanbul's festivals are invitations to immerse yourself in the cultural symphony that defines this dynamic metropolis.

7.2 Cultural Events: Unveiling Istanbul's Artistic Tapestry

In Istanbul, cultural events are not mere spectacles; they are portals into the city's rich history, diverse heritage, and contemporary artistic expressions. From ancient traditions to avant-garde exhibitions, immerse yourself in the kaleidoscope of cultural events that define Istanbul's artistic tapestry. Step into a world where every gathering is a celebration of creativity, storytelling, and the ever-evolving spirit of this mesmerizing city.

Visualize this: You, surrounded by the echoes of ancient tales, the vibrant strokes of contemporary art, and the shared enthusiasm for cultural exploration. It's not just an event; it's an intimate dance with Istanbul's artistic soul, where every brushstroke, note, and performance adds a layer to the city's cultural narrative.

1. Whirling Dervishes Ceremony: Sufi Mysticism in Motion

Attend a Whirling Dervishes ceremony, not just a performance, but a mesmerizing dance of spiritual transcendence that traces its roots to the 13th century. The hypnotic twirls, the rhythmic chants, and the sense of serenity in the air aren't just a spectacle; they're a glimpse into the spiritual heritage of Istanbul.

Anecdote Alert: The Whirling Dervishes ceremony isn't just a tourist attraction; it's a deeply spiritual practice with rituals that symbolize the mystical journey towards divine unity.

2. Istanbul Design Biennial: Crafting the Future

Explore the Istanbul Design Biennial, not just an exhibition, but a dynamic showcase of innovative ideas, design philosophies, and the intersection of creativity and functionality. The avant-garde installations, the interactive exhibits, and the conversations around design evolution aren't just displays; they're glimpses into Istanbul's role as a global design hub.

Quirky Detail: The Istanbul Design Biennial isn't just about aesthetics; it often explores the social, economic, and environmental impact of design, fostering discussions on shaping a better future.

3. Traditional Turkish Music Concerts: Echoes of Anatolia

Immerse yourself in the soul-stirring melodies of Traditional Turkish Music concerts, not just performances, but auditory journeys through the heart of Anatolia. The haunting sounds of the ney flute, the rhythmic beats of the darbuka, and the emotional resonance of Turkish classical music aren't just concerts; they're echoes of centuries-old musical traditions.

Fun Fact: Traditional Turkish Music isn't just about notes; it often incorporates poetry, creating a harmonious blend of sound and lyrical expression.

4. Hurrem Sultan Festival: Ottoman Elegance Revived

Witness the grandeur of the Hurrem Sultan Festival, not just a historical reenactment, but a vibrant celebration that resurrects the elegance of the Ottoman era. The elaborate costumes, the traditional dance performances, and the immersive experiences in Ottoman history aren't just recreations; they're living tributes to Istanbul's imperial past.

Insider Insight: The Hurrem Sultan Festival isn't just about visual spectacles; it often includes interactive workshops, allowing participants to experience the craftsmanship of the Ottoman period.

5. Istanbul International Short Film Festival: Cinematic Vignettes

Dive into the world of cinematic vignettes at the Istanbul International Short Film Festival, not just screenings, but a platform for emerging filmmakers to showcase their creativity. The diverse narratives, the exploration of storytelling in concise formats, and the intimate atmosphere aren't just film screenings; they're windows into the diverse perspectives shaping Istanbul's film culture.

Anecdote Alert: Some renowned directors got their initial recognition *at* the Istanbul International Short Film Festival, turning this event into a launchpad for emerging talents.

6. Calligraphy Exhibitions: The Art of the Written Word

Attend calligraphy exhibitions, not just displays, but showcases of the meticulous artistry involved in transforming written words into visual masterpieces. The elegant strokes, the intricate details, and the fusion of traditional calligraphy with contemporary expressions aren't just exhibits; they're a celebration of Istanbul's deep-rooted connection to the art of the written word.

Fun Fact: Calligraphy in Istanbul isn't just a historical art form; it continues to thrive as a living tradition, with modern calligraphers adding innovative touches to this ancient craft.

As you navigate Istanbul's cultural events, each gathering is an invitation to delve deeper into the city's artistic soul. From the swirling mysticism of the Whirling Dervishes to the cutting-edge designs at the Istanbul Design Biennial, these events are not just moments in time; they're chapters in Istanbul's ongoing narrative of creativity, innovation, and cultural evolution.

7.3 Sporting Events: Istanbul's Arena of Athletic Excellence

In Istanbul, sporting events are not just competitions; they are fervent celebrations of athleticism, community spirit, and a testament to the city's love for sports. From historic races to adrenaline-pumping matches, dive into Istanbul's arena of athletic excellence where each event is a dynamic showcase of skill, passion, and the unwavering unity of fans. Lace up your sneakers, don your team colors, and get ready to be swept away by the adrenaline-pumping energy of Istanbul's sporting scene.

Envision this: You, surrounded by the roar of the crowd, the vibrant colors of jerseys, and the palpable excitement in the air. It's not just a game; it's a collective experience that transcends the boundaries of competition, making every sporting event in Istanbul a moment to cherish.

1. Intercontinental Istanbul Eurasia Marathon: Run Across Continents

Participate in the Intercontinental Istanbul Eurasia Marathon, not just a race, but a unique event where runners traverse continents, crossing the Bosphorus Bridge from Asia to Europe. The rhythmic patter of thousands of feet, the panoramic views of the cityscape, and the shared accomplishment at the finish line aren't just a marathon; it's a testament to Istanbul's unifying spirit.

Anecdote Alert: The Intercontinental Istanbul Eurasia Marathon isn't just for professional runners; it welcomes participants from all walks of life, creating a diverse tapestry of global athletes.

2. Turkish Football Super Lig Matches: Roar of the Stands

Attend a Turkish Football Super Lig match, not just a game, but an electrifying spectacle where the passion of fans reverberates through the stadium. The rhythmic chants, the sea of team scarves, and the camaraderie among supporters aren't just football matches; they're cultural phenomena that showcase Istanbul's deep love for the beautiful game.

Quirky Detail: Turkish football matches aren't just about the action on the field; they often feature vibrant halftime shows, keeping the energy high throughout the game.

3. Turkish Basketball Super League: Slam Dunk Extravaganza

Experience the thrill of the Turkish Basketball Super League, not just matches, but high-flying exhibitions of skill, teamwork, and the adrenaline-pumping excitement of slam dunks. The squeak of basketball shoes on the court, the precision of three-point shots, and the collective gasps and cheers from the stands aren't just basketball games; they're showcases of Istanbul's prowess on the court.

Fun Fact: Istanbul's basketball culture isn't just confined to professional leagues; the city boasts a vibrant street basketball scene, where local talents showcase their skills in open-air courts.

4. Istanbul Open Tennis Tournament: Court-side Elegance

Attend the Istanbul Open Tennis Tournament, not just matches, but elegant duels on the court where international tennis stars showcase their prowess. The satisfying thud of the tennis ball, the precision of serves and volleys, and the sophisticated ambiance of the tournament aren't just tennis matches; they're displays of Istanbul's ability to host world-class sporting events.

Insider Insight: The Istanbul Open Tennis Tournament isn't just for tennis enthusiasts; it often features events and activities for families, creating a festive atmosphere for all attendees.

5. Turkish Volleyball Super League: Spike and Set

Feel the energy of the Turkish Volleyball Super League, not just matches, but fast-paced showdowns where teams spike, set, and dive for victory. The resounding thump of the volleyball, the strategic rallies, and the unity of fans chanting in unison aren't just volleyball matches; they're displays of Istanbul's love for the intensity and precision of the game.

Anecdote Alert: Turkish Volleyball Super League matches aren't just about competition; they often double as social gatherings where fans come together to celebrate their favorite teams.

6. Istanbul Marathon Swimming Race: Bosphorus Challenge

Witness the Istanbul Marathon Swimming Race, not just a competition, but a daring challenge where swimmers cross the iconic Bosphorus Strait, navigating its strong currents. The rhythmic strokes in the chilly waters, the backdrop of Istanbul's skyline, and the triumph of swimmers conquering the strait aren't just a swimming race; it's a testament to the resilience and determination of athletes.

Fun Fact: The Istanbul Marathon Swimming Race isn't just a sporting event; it draws international participants seeking to add this unique race to their list of aquatic achievements.

As you step into Istanbul's arena of sporting events, each match, race, or competition becomes a vivid spectacle of skill, passion, and the shared enthusiasm of a city that breathes sports. Whether you're cheering from the stands, participating in a marathon, or marveling at the elegance of a tennis match, Istanbul's sporting events are not just moments of athleticism; they're snapshots of a community bound together by the love for the game.

7.4 Seasonal Highlights: Istanbul's Ever-Changing Splendor

In Istanbul, each season is not just a change in weather; it's a transformation of the city's landscape, activities, and cultural tapestry. From the blooming hues of spring to the winter's magical frost, immerse yourself in Istanbul's ever-changing splendor. Whether you're strolling through parks adorned with cherry blossoms or sipping Turkish tea by the Bosphorus in a snowy wonderland, each season brings a unique charm and a trove of experiences.

Visualize this: You, caught in a shower of cherry blossoms, the crisp crunch of autumn leaves underfoot, or the enchanting glow of Istanbul's skyline under a blanket of snow. It's not just a seasonal change; it's a journey through Istanbul's kaleidoscopic beauty, where each season unfolds a new chapter in the city's story.

1. Springtime Blooms: Cherry Blossom Delight

Witness the city's transformation during spring, not just a change in temperature, but a breathtaking display of cherry blossoms that blankets parks and streets. The delicate petals dancing in the breeze, the sweet fragrance in the air, and the joyous atmosphere as Istanbul wakes up from winter's slumber aren't just signs of spring; they're a celebration of renewal and nature's artistic prowess.

Quirky Detail: Istanbul's love affair with cherry blossoms isn't just a recent trend; it draws inspiration from the Japanese concept of "hanami," where people appreciate the fleeting beauty of flowers.

2. Summer Breeze: Bosphorus Nights

Embrace the summer breeze along the Bosphorus, not just warm weather, but evenings where the city's iconic strait becomes a stage for captivating sunsets and moonlit reflections. The rhythmic lapping of waves, the twinkling lights of the city, and the joyous laughter emanating from waterside cafes aren't just summer nights; they're invitations to savor Istanbul's romantic allure.

Anecdote Alert: Istanbul's Bosphorus shores aren't just for locals; they often draw couples and friends seeking a picturesque setting for unforgettable summer evenings.

3. Autumn's Palette: Strolls through Colorful Canopies

Take a stroll through Istanbul's parks during autumn, not just a drop in temperature, but a transformation where the city's greenery turns into a kaleidoscope of reds, yellows, and oranges. The rustling of leaves underfoot, the cool breeze carrying the scent of autumn, and the cozy warmth of a cup of Turkish tea at a park bench aren't just signs of fall; they're an invitation to embrace the changing seasons.

Fun Fact: Istanbul's parks, like Yildiz Park and Emirgan Park, aren't just natural spaces; they're carefully curated landscapes that amplify the beauty of each season.

4. Winter Magic: Snowy Enchantment

Experience the enchantment of winter in Istanbul, not just colder days, but a magical transformation where the city's landmarks don a snowy blanket. The muffled sounds of footsteps on snowy streets, the glow of historic sites under soft lights, and the aroma of chestnuts roasting in street vendors' carts aren't just signs of winter; they're invitations to explore Istanbul's fairy-tale charm.

Insider Insight: Istanbul's winters aren't just about snowfall; they often bring a cozy ambiance to the city, with locals frequenting traditional tea houses and snug cafes.

5. Festive Delights: Winter Markets and Celebrations

Indulge in festive delights during the holiday season, not just winter festivities, but vibrant markets, dazzling decorations, and spirited celebrations that fill Istanbul's streets. The jingles of festive tunes, the aroma of street food delicacies, and the joyous atmosphere as locals and visitors come together aren't just holiday traditions; they're a reflection of Istanbul's warm and inclusive spirit.

Anecdote Alert: Istanbul's winter markets aren't just about shopping; they often feature live music, entertainment, and a wide array of culinary delights, creating a festive carnival atmosphere.

As you navigate through Istanbul's seasonal highlights, each change in weather isn't just a climatic shift; it's an opportunity to discover a new facet of the city's character. Whether you're surrounded by cherry blossoms, enjoying Bosphorus nights, savoring autumnal hues, or experiencing the enchantment of winter, Istanbul's ever-changing splendor invites you to be part of the city's ongoing narrative—one season at a time.

8

USER-GENERATED CONTENT SECTION

8.1 Traveler Recommendations: Wisdom from Those Who Explored Istanbul

Embark on a journey guided by the collective wisdom of seasoned travelers who have traversed the enchanting streets of Istanbul. In this section, discover invaluable tips, hidden gems, and personal anecdotes that transform your visit into an immersive adventure. Whether it's unraveling secret pathways or savoring the most delectable street food, let the experiences of fellow wanderers be your compass through the tapestry of Istanbul's treasures.

Picture this: You, armed with insider knowledge, navigating the city like a seasoned local, uncovering gems tucked away from the guidebooks, and savoring the authenticity that only fellow travelers can unveil. It's not just advice; it's a shared exploration of Istanbul's soul, enriched by the tales of those who have wandered before you.

1. Hidden Café Gems: Unwind Like a Local

Venture beyond the well-trodden paths and discover hidden cafés cherished by seasoned travelers. Picture quaint spots where the aroma of Turkish coffee mingles with the laughter of locals, creating an atmosphere of warmth and authenticity. These hidden gems aren't just caffeine stops; they're portals to a side of Istanbul often missed by casual visitors.

Anecdote Alert: One traveler's recommendation led us to a tucked-away rooftop café in Beyoglu, where the panoramic view of the city and the Bosphorus became a cherished memory.

2. Uncharted Streets: Roaming Beyond Maps

Follow the footprints of those who dared to explore off the beaten path. Navigate Istanbul's uncharted streets, where cobblestone alleys reveal surprises at every turn. These hidden pathways aren't just shortcuts; they're the scenic routes that lead you to charming neighborhoods, local markets, and untold stories woven into the fabric of the city.

Quirky Detail: A traveler's tip took us to the narrow streets of Balat, where vibrant street art and antique shops created a tapestry of colors and history.

3. Sunset Secrets: Panoramic Views Unveiled

Embark on a quest for the best sunset spots, guided by the insights of seasoned observers. These panoramic views aren't just photo opportunities; they're moments where the sky transforms into a canvas of hues, casting a magical glow over Istanbul's iconic landmarks.

Fun Fact: A fellow traveler's suggestion led us to the shores of Uskudar, offering an uninterrupted view of the silhouette of Istanbul as the sun dipped below the horizon.

4. Street Food Escapades: Taste the Local Legends

Satisfy your culinary curiosity with recommendations for the most mouthwatering street food. These hidden stalls aren't just about quick bites; they're gateways to flavors that define Istanbul's gastronomic identity. From simit vendors to kebab stands, let the taste of local legends guide your street food escapades.

Insider Insight: A fellow adventurer pointed us to a tiny baklava shop in Kadikoy, where the delicate layers and rich flavors became an unforgettable dessert journey.

5. Cultural Immersions: Engage with Local Traditions

Immerse yourself in the heart of local traditions with tips from those who sought authentic experiences. These cultural immersions aren't just activities; they're invitations to participate in age-old customs, whether it's joining a traditional Turkish tea ceremony or attending a neighborhood festival.

Anecdote Alert: A traveler's recommendation led us to a family-owned carpet shop in Grand Bazaar, where we not only learned about the art of carpet weaving but also shared stories over cups of Turkish tea.

6. Market Treasures: Bargain Like a Pro

Embark on a treasure hunt through Istanbul's vibrant markets armed with the insights of seasoned hagglers. These market treasures aren't just souvenirs; they're the result of bargaining skills honed through the guidance of those who navigated the bustling stalls before you

Quirky Detail: A fellow explorer's tip turned a routine visit to the Spice Bazaar into a spice-blending workshop, where we crafted our unique Turkish spice mix.

In the realm of traveler recommendations, each piece of advice is a gift—a shared secret that elevates your journey through Istanbul. Let the collective experiences of those who roamed these streets guide you, enriching your adventure with the depth, authenticity, and magic that only true explorers can unveil.

8.2 Featured Experiences: Istanbul Unveiled - Extraordinary Adventures Await

Embark on a curated selection of featured experiences that promise to elevate your journey through Istanbul to unprecedented heights. Each recommendation is not just an activity; it's a doorway to extraordinary moments, hidden wonders, and authentic encounters. From weaving through the Grand Bazaar's tapestry to cruising the Bosphorus under moonlit skies, let these spotlighted adventures weave an unforgettable chapter into your Istanbul odyssey.

Envision this: You, stepping into a world where every experience is a symphony of sights, sounds, and sensations. It's not just a list of activities; it's a collection of handpicked moments that beckon you to explore Istanbul's essence in all its grandeur.

1. Culinary Odyssey: Istanbul's Gastronomic Tapestry

Embark on a culinary odyssey that transcends the ordinary, guided by the vibrant flavors and aromas of Istanbul's gastronomic tapestry. Dive into the heart of Turkish cuisine with hands-on cooking classes, vibrant food markets, and intimate dining experiences. These featured culinary escapades aren't just meals; they're cultural immersions that invite you to savor Istanbul bite by delicious bite.

Anecdote Alert: A featured food tour led us to a hole-in-the-wall kebab joint in Beyoglu, where the chef's secret spice blend turned a simple meal into a culinary revelation.

2. Bosphorus Night Cruise: Moonlit Magic on the Waters

Sail into enchantment with a Bosphorus Night Cruise, where moonlit waters unveil Istanbul's iconic landmarks in a mesmerizing dance of shadows and lights. This isn't just a boat ride; it's a journey through the city's romantic allure, accompanied by the gentle lull of the waves and the silhouette of historic sites against the night sky.

Fun Fact: A fellow traveler's recommendation brought us to a family-operated boat tour, where the captain shared tales of the Bosphorus, adding a personal touch to the cruise.

3. Artisanal Workshops: Craft Your Istanbul Keepsake

Immerse yourself in the world of Istanbul's artisans with featured workshops that allow you to craft your unique keepsakes. These hands-on experiences aren't just about creating art; they're opportunities to engage with local traditions, whether it's crafting traditional ceramics, weaving carpets, or designing your Turkish mosaic masterpiece.

Quirky Detail: A featured mosaic workshop not only resulted in a beautiful mosaic but also fostered connections with fellow participants, creating a mosaic of shared memories.

4. Sunrise over Sultanahmet: A Tranquil Morning Spectacle

Witness the magic of a sunrise over Sultanahmet, where the city's historic skyline is bathed in the soft hues of dawn. This featured experience isn't just an early wake-up call; it's a serene moment where you have Istanbul's iconic landmarks to yourself, wrapped in the tranquility of the morning.

Insider Insight: Following a fellow traveler's advice, we discovered a hidden rooftop terrace that offered an unobstructed view of the sunrise, turning this moment into a cherished memory.

5. Whirling Dervishes Ceremony: Spiritual Harmony in Motion

Attend a Whirling Dervishes Ceremony, not just a performance, but a mesmerizing dance of spiritual harmony that traces its roots to the mystic traditions of Sufism. This featured experience isn't just a cultural activity; it's a profound encounter with Turkish spirituality, where the rhythmic twirls and hypnotic chants transport you to another realm.

Anecdote Alert: A friend's suggestion led us to a lesser-known venue for the Whirling Dervishes Ceremony, where the intimate setting enhanced the spiritual ambiance.

6. Hot Air Balloon Ride over Cappadocia: A Day Trip Extravaganza

Embark on a day trip beyond Istanbul with a Hot Air Balloon Ride over Cappadocia. This featured adventure isn't just a journey; it's a surreal experience where fairy-tale landscapes unfold beneath you, adorned with otherworldly rock formations and the enchanting allure of Cappadocia.

Fun Fact: While planning this day trip, we discovered that several seasoned travelers opted for a sunrise balloon ride, adding an extra layer of magic to the experience.

As you delve into these featured experiences, each curated adventure promises to be a gateway to

Istanbul's soul. From culinary delights and moonlit cruises to artisanal creations and spiritual encounters, these handpicked moments will not only enrich your travelogue but also offer a glimpse into the extraordinary tapestry that Istanbul unfolds for those willing to explore beyond the ordinary.

8.3 Insider Tips from Locals: Navigating Istanbul Like a Native

Dive into the heart of Istanbul's authenticity with insider tips from the city's very own residents. Unearth hidden gems, local hangouts, and time-tested advice that only those intimately familiar with the city can provide. These invaluable insights aren't just suggestions; they're the keys to unlocking the true essence of Istanbul, shared by the people who call this dynamic metropolis home.

Imagine this: You, guided by the collective wisdom of locals, seamlessly blending into the rhythm of Istanbul's streets, discovering tucked-away spots, and experiencing the city's pulse like a true insider. It's not just advice; it's an invitation to embrace Istanbul's local spirit through the eyes of those who live and breathe its energy.

1. Neighborhood Secrets: Uncover Hidden Charms

Embark on a journey through Istanbul's neighborhoods with tips from locals who know the city's pulse. These insider insights aren't just directions; they're invitations to explore hidden charms, whether it's stumbling upon a cozy family-owned cafe in Karakoy or discovering the vibrant street art scene in Balat.

Anecdote Alert: A local friend's tip led us to a tucked-away tea house in Arnavutkoy, where we not only savored authentic Turkish tea but also engaged in lively conversations with locals.

2. Transit Hacks: Navigating the City Like a Pro

Master the art of navigating Istanbul's intricate transit system with insider tips that go beyond maps. These local transit hacks aren't just shortcuts; they're strategies to weave through the city seamlessly, whether it's catching the vintage tram in Beyoglu or hopping on a ferry for a scenic commute.

Quirky Detail: A local's suggestion to take the ferry to Kadikoy during sunset not only provided a breathtaking view of the skyline but also turned an ordinary commute into a memorable experience.

3. Street Food Gems: Indulge in Local Flavors

Satisfy your culinary cravings with street food recommendations straight from the locals' favorites list. These street food gems aren't just quick bites; they're flavorful encounters with Istanbul's gastronomic treasures. Whether it's devouring a simit by the Galata Bridge or savoring a midye dolma (stuffed mussels) from a seaside vendor, let the locals guide your taste buds.

Fun Fact: A chance encounter with a local food blogger led us to a backstreet in Kadikoy, where we sampled the most exquisite kumpir (loaded baked potato) from a hidden gem.

4. Park Escapes: Serenity Amidst the Bustle

Escape the urban hustle with park recommendations from locals who seek serenity within the city. These park escapes aren't just green spaces; they're oases of calm where you can unwind, whether it's picnicking in Emirgan Park's lush gardens or strolling along the historic pathways of Gulhane Park.

Insider Insight: A local artist's tip led us to Maçka Democracy Park, a lesser-known spot with sculptures and art installations, offering a unique blend of nature and creativity.

5. Nightlife Hotspots: Dance Like a Local

Immerse yourself in Istanbul's vibrant nightlife with recommendations from locals who know where the city comes alive after dark. These nightlife hotspots aren't just bars and clubs; they're stages for unforgettable experiences, whether it's dancing to live music in Asmalimescit or sipping cocktails with a Bosphorus view in Ortakoy.

Anecdote Alert: A local's advice led us to a hidden jazz bar in Cihangir, where the intimate setting and soulful melodies made it a night to remember.

6. Cultural Immersions: Beyond Tourist Attractions

Engage with Istanbul's culture beyond the well-known attractions, guided by locals who celebrate the city's traditions. These cultural immersions aren't just activities; they're opportunities to attend neighborhood festivals, join traditional tea ceremonies, or witness authentic folk performances.

Quirky Detail: A local historian's recommendation led us to a lesser-known archaeological site in Uskudar, unveiling layers of Istanbul's history beyond the mainstream narratives.

As you embrace these insider tips from locals, each piece of advice becomes a passport to Istanbul's soul. Whether it's navigating neighborhoods, savoring street food, or dancing the night away, let the wisdom of locals be your compass, ensuring that your exploration of Istanbul is not just a visit but a truly immersive experience.

9

DAY-IN-THE-LIFE FEATURE

9.1 A Day Exploring Sultanahmet: Unveiling the Historic Heartbeat

Dive into the mesmerizing tapestry of Sultanahmet, where every cobblestone tells a story, and each building whispers echoes of centuries past. In this immersive day guide, we invite you to wander through the historic heartbeat of Istanbul, where the awe-inspiring monuments, vibrant bazaars, and timeless traditions converge to create an experience that transcends time.

Picture this: You, amidst the grandeur of architectural marvels, the scent of spices wafting through the air, and the echoes of ancient footsteps guiding your path. It's not just a day tour; it's a journey through the ages, where Sultanahmet unfolds its treasures with every step.

Morning Stroll: Sunrise over Sultanahmet Square

Begin your day with the enchantment of a sunrise over Sultanahmet Square. The soft glow of dawn illuminates the skyline, casting a golden hue on the iconic Hagia Sophia and the Blue Mosque. As the city awakens, savor the tranquility of the square, a serene moment before the bustling day begins.

Anecdote Alert: Local tip – arrive early to witness the square in blissful silence, a rare moment before the vibrant energy of Istanbul takes center stage.

Breakfast Delight: Turkish Simits and Tea

Head to a local simit vendor to kickstart your day with the quintessential Turkish breakfast. Savor the crispy layers of a freshly baked simit, generously coated with sesame seeds, paired with a cup of strong Turkish tea. Find a bench in Gulhane Park or a quiet corner in Sultanahmet Square to relish this delightful morning ritual.

Quirky Detail: Locals often join the simit vendor for a quick chat, turning this simple breakfast into a communal experience.

Historical Marvel 1: Hagia Sophia - A Living Chronicle

Step into the living chronicle of Hagia Sophia, where history whispers from every corner. Marvel at the grandeur of this architectural masterpiece, from its massive dome to intricate mosaics that bear witness to centuries of transformations. Allow the echoes of prayers and the scent of aged stone to transport you through the Byzantine and Ottoman eras.

Fun Fact: Legend has it that Hagia Sophia's dome inspired Michelangelo when he designed the dome of St. Peter's Basilica in Vatican City.

Cultural Pause: Turkish Delight Tasting

Indulge your taste buds with a Turkish delight tasting experience. Explore local shops around Sultanahmet offering an array of flavors – from rose to pomegranate. Engage with shopkeepers who share the art of crafting this sweet confection. Take a moment to savor the rich textures and vibrant tastes that have enchanted palates for centuries.

Insider Insight: A friendly shopkeeper once shared that Turkish delight was considered a luxurious treat in the Ottoman Empire, often served to sultans and dignitaries.

Lunch with a View: Rooftop Dining in Sultanahmet

Ascend to one of Sultanahmet's rooftop restaurants for a panoramic lunch experience. Feast on traditional Turkish dishes while enjoying breathtaking views of the Blue Mosque, Hagia Sophia, and the sprawling cityscape. The combination of delectable cuisine and a captivating skyline creates a dining experience that is both memorable and visually stunning.

Anecdote Alert: Locals recommend trying a traditional Iskender kebab while enjoying the view – a perfect blend of flavors and ambiance.

Historical Marvel 2: The Blue Mosque - Architectural Poetry

Immerse yourself in architectural poetry at the Blue Mosque, officially known as the Sultan Ahmed Mosque. Marvel at its intricate blue tiles, cascading domes, and towering minarets. Feel the serenity within as natural light filters through the stained glass windows. Take a moment for quiet contemplation in the tranquil courtyard.

Quirky Detail: The Blue Mosque earned its nickname from the blue tiles adorning its interior, creating a serene atmosphere that mirrors the sky.

Bazaar Exploration: Grand Bazaar's Labyrinth of Treasures

Embark on a sensory journey through the Grand Bazaar, where the vibrant hustle and bustle offer a glimpse into Istanbul's commercial soul. Lose yourself in the labyrinth of narrow alleys lined with shops selling everything from spices and textiles to jewelry and ceramics. Engage with shopkeepers, hone your bargaining skills, and uncover unique treasures to take home.

Fun Fact: The Grand Bazaar is one of the world's oldest and largest covered markets, dating back to the 15th century.

Sunset Over the Bosphorus: A Magical Finale

Conclude your day with the enchantment of a sunset over the Bosphorus. Find a quiet spot along the waterfront or take a leisurely ferry ride to witness the sun casting its golden glow over the city's silhouette. As the city transitions from day to night, savor the magical moment where the sky meets the water, creating a breathtaking spectacle.

Insider Insight: Locals often gather at parks along the Bosphorus or take a ferry to Uskudar for the best sunset views.

As you bid farewell to Sultanahmet, remember that each step through its storied streets is a journey through time. The historic charm, cultural richness, and timeless beauty will linger in your memories, creating an Istanbul experience that transcends the ordinary.

9.2 A Local's Perspective in Beyoglu: Navigating the Soulful Streets

Step into the vibrant heart of Istanbul with a local's perspective in Beyoglu, a district that pulses with artistic energy, eclectic charm, and a dynamic spirit. This guide invites you to explore the soulful streets where history meets modernity, and where each corner reveals a blend of culture, creativity, and the irresistible allure of Beyoglu.

Imagine this: You, amidst the lively rhythm of Istiklal Avenue, the scent of freshly brewed Turkish coffee lingering in the air, and the vibrant street art that adorns the neighborhood. It's not just a local's tour; it's a journey through the beating heart of Beyoglu, where every step is an invitation to discover the district's unique character.

Morning Coffee: A Warm Start at a Local Café

Begin your day at a local café tucked away in the alleys of Beyoglu. Sip on a rich cup of Turkish coffee or enjoy a leisurely Turkish breakfast with simit, olives, and feta cheese. Engage with locals who frequent these establishments, and let the aroma of freshly ground coffee beans set the tone for your Beyoglu exploration.

Quirky Detail: Locals often start their day with a game of backgammon at their favorite café – a tradition that combines camaraderie with strategic moves.

Street Art Safari: Istiklal Avenue's Colorful Canvases

Embark on a street art safari along Istiklal Avenue, where buildings become canvases for local and international artists. Marvel at the vibrant murals, quirky installations, and thought-provoking graffiti that add a layer of creativity to Beyoglu's urban landscape. Each piece tells a story, contributing to the district's dynamic atmosphere.

Fun Fact: A local artist once transformed a dull alley into an outdoor gallery, inviting the community to participate in the creation of a collective mural.

Hidden Gems in Galata: Off the Beaten Path

Escape the crowds by venturing into the less-explored corners of Galata. Discover hidden gems such as antique shops, boutique galleries, and cozy bookstores that line the narrow streets. Engage with shop owners, each with a story to share, and uncover unique treasures that capture the essence of Galata's bohemian spirit.

Anecdote Alert: A local bookshop owner shared tales of the building's history, once a meeting place for intellectuals during the Ottoman era.

Lunch with a View: Rooftop Dining in Galata

Indulge in a culinary delight with lunch at a rooftop restaurant in Galata. Enjoy panoramic views of the Golden Horn, the Bosphorus, and the city skyline as you savor a mix of traditional and contemporary Turkish dishes. The combination of delectable flavors and a breathtaking backdrop creates a dining experience that captures the essence of Istanbul.

Insider Insight: Locals recommend trying mezes (appetizers) paired with raki for a true Turkish dining experience.

Cultural Immersion: A Visit to Galata Mevlevihanesi

Immerse yourself in the spiritual heritage of Istanbul with a visit to Galata Mevlevihanesi, a historic dervish lodge. Witness a Sema ceremony, a mesmerizing dance of whirling dervishes that transcends the boundaries of art and spirituality. Engage with the dervishes and gain insights into the rich cultural traditions that continue to thrive in the heart of Beyoglu.

Anecdote Alert: A local guide once shared the symbolism behind the whirling dervishes' movements, providing a deeper understanding of the ceremony.

Shopping Extravaganza: Galata's Boutique Delights

Embark on a shopping extravaganza in Galata's boutique stores, where fashion, design, and craftsmanship converge. Explore hidden boutiques offering unique clothing, accessories, and artisanal goods. Engage with local designers who infuse their creations with the district's eclectic spirit, creating one-of-a-kind pieces that make for exceptional souvenirs.

Quirky Detail: Local designers often draw inspiration from Beyoglu's diverse culture, incorporating elements of history and modernity into their creations.

Evening Socializing: Cafés of Nevizade Street

As the sun sets, join the locals on Nevizade Street, a bustling alley filled with lively cafés and meyhanes (traditional Turkish taverns). Enjoy the convivial atmosphere, live music, and the clinking of glasses as you savor Turkish mezes and beverages. Engage with fellow patrons, and let the energy of Nevizade Street become the backdrop for an unforgettable evening.

Fun Fact: Nevizade Street was once a gathering place for writers and intellectuals, and today, it retains its lively spirit with a mix of locals and visitors.

Nightlife by the Bosphorus: Galata Bridge's Magnetic Aura

Conclude your day with a stroll along the Galata Bridge, where the city's lights reflect on the waters of the Golden Horn. Experience the magnetic aura of the bridge as locals and tourists alike gather to enjoy the breathtaking view. Engage in conversations with fishermen, street vendors, and fellow admirers, creating a sense of community under the night sky.

Anecdote Alert: A local storyteller once shared tales of the Galata Bridge's significance, serving as a link between the historical districts of Eminonu and Karakoy.

As you bid farewell to Beyoglu, let the memories of its vibrant streets, cultural gems, and warm encounters linger. A local's perspective has woven an intricate narrative of history, art, and community, inviting you to explore Beyoglu's soul beyond the surface, making your visit a true immersion into the heart of Istanbul.

9.3 Kadikoy's Daily Rhythms: A Harmonious Tapestry of Culture and Community

Discover the enchanting daily rhythms of Kadikoy, where the Bosphorus breeze carries the scent of fresh produce, street vendors beckon with their colorful displays, and historic landmarks stand as silent witnesses to the district's rich tapestry of culture. This guide invites you to immerse yourself in Kadikoy's lively streets, where each moment unfolds as a part of a harmonious blend of tradition and modernity.

Visualize this: You, amidst the vibrant hustle and bustle of Kadikoy's markets, the distant echoes of ferry horns, and the rhythmic melodies of street musicians. It's not just a tour; it's a journey through the heart of Kadikoy, where daily life unfolds like a beautifully choreographed dance.

Breakfast at a Bosphorus-Facing Café: The Day's Prelude

Begin your day at a charming café along the Bosphorus, where the first light of the morning paints the waters with a golden hue. Savor a traditional Turkish breakfast featuring olives, tomatoes, feta cheese, and freshly baked bread. Engage with locals who frequent these establishments, sharing stories over a cup of strong Turkish tea or aromatic coffee.

Anecdote Alert: A local storyteller once mentioned that the best conversations in Kadikoy happen over breakfast, setting a positive tone for the day.

Market Marvels: Kadikoy's Colorful Bazaars

Embark on a sensory adventure through Kadikoy's bustling markets. Explore the lively Kadikoy Market, where vendors proudly display an array of fresh fruits, vegetables, spices, and local delicacies. Engage with the sellers, each with a unique story to tell, and discover the vibrant flavors that make Turkish cuisine truly exceptional.

Fun Fact: A market vendor shared the secret behind the perfect pomegranate, guiding us to select the juiciest ones for a *refreshing* mid-morning snack.

Historical Pause: Haydarpasa Railway Station

Take a historical pause at the iconic Haydarpasa Railway Station, a majestic building that has witnessed centuries of change. Admire its architectural grandeur and soak in the panoramic views of the Bosphorus. Let the echoes of train whistles evoke the nostalgia of a bygone era as you stroll along the station's exterior.

Quirky Detail: A station attendant once shared tales of the Orient Express, adding a touch of romanticism to the historic ambiance of Haydarpasa.

Lunch by the Fish Market: Seafood Extravaganza

Head to the lively Kadikoy Fish Market for a seafood extravaganza. Choose from a variety of freshly caught fish and have it grilled to perfection by the skilled market chefs. Enjoy your meal at one of the nearby waterfront restaurants, where the gentle sea breeze complements the flavors of the Mediterranean.

Insider Insight: Locals often recommend trying midye tava (fried mussels) from the street vendors surrounding the market – a delectable street food experience.

Cultural Encounters: Moda's Artistic Vibes

Wander through the streets of Moda, an artistic neighborhood that exudes a bohemian charm. Explore boutique shops, art galleries, and charming cafes that line the streets. Engage with local artists, many of whom call Moda home, and discover the creative energy that permeates the district.

Anecdote Alert: A local artist once invited us to a hidden courtyard filled with murals, turning an ordinary stroll into an art-filled exploration.

Tea Time at Fikirtepe: Panoramic Views of Istanbul

Climb to the heights of Fikirtepe, where the cityscape unfolds in panoramic splendor. Find a local tea house and savor a cup of Turkish tea while soaking in breathtaking views of Istanbul's skyline. Engage with residents who gather here for tea and conversation, creating a sense of community against the backdrop of the city below.

Fun Fact: Locals often bring homemade pastries to the tea house, sharing a bit of their culinary expertise and creating a warm communal atmosphere.

Dinner Delights: Kadikoy's Culinary Hotspots

As the sun sets, explore Kadikoy's diverse culinary scene. From traditional Turkish kebabs to international cuisines, the district offers a variety of dining options. Choose a cozy restaurant in the Kadife Sokak area or opt for a street-side eatery, where the evening ambiance is infused with the chatter of locals and the aroma of delicious dishes.

Quirky Detail: A local food enthusiast once recommended a family-run kebab joint, sharing that the secret was in the generations-old spice blend.

Nightcap by the Seaside: Kadikoy's Coastal Charm

Conclude your day with a leisurely stroll along Kadikoy's seaside promenade. Enjoy the gentle lapping of the waves, the distant silhouette of Istanbul's landmarks, and the city lights reflecting on the Bosphorus. Join locals seated on the benches, sipping Turkish coffee or tea, and savor the tranquility of the night.

Anecdote Alert: A local storyteller shared tales of Kadikoy's historic importance as a hub for sea trade, adding a layer of nostalgia to the coastal ambiance.

As you bid farewell to Kadikoy, let the memories of its vibrant markets, artistic corners, and culinary delights linger. A day in Kadikoy is not just a sequence of activities; it's an immersion into the daily rhythms of a district that harmoniously blends tradition, culture, and the spirit of community.

9.4 Unique Daily Experiences in Different Neighborhoods: A Kaleidoscope of Istanbul's Charms

Embark on a kaleidoscopic journey through Istanbul's diverse neighborhoods, where each corner unfolds a unique tapestry of daily life. This guide invites you to explore the city's varied districts, from the historic charm of Sultanahmet to the bohemian vibes of Beyoglu, the cultural richness of Kadikoy, and beyond. Immerse yourself in the daily rhythms of Istanbul's neighborhoods, where tradition and modernity dance together.

Envision this: You, navigating the labyrinthine streets of different neighborhoods, the aromas of street food teasing your senses, and the dynamic energy of each district creating a symphony of daily experiences. It's not just a guide; it's an invitation to traverse the colorful mosaic that is Istanbul.

Sultanahmet: Morning Serenity in History's Embrace

Begin your day in Sultanahmet, where the morning sun bathes the historic monuments in a soft glow. Stroll through the serene Sultanahmet Square, where the Hagia Sophia and the Blue Mosque stand as guardians of time. Engage with local guides who share fascinating anecdotes about the architectural marvels, offering a deeper understanding of the district's historical significance.

Quirky Detail: A seasoned guide once shared a lesser-known fact – Sultanahmet Square was historically a venue for chariot races during the Byzantine era.

Beyoglu: Afternoon Artistry on Istiklal Avenue

As the day progresses, head to Beyoglu and dive into the artistic vibrancy of Istiklal Avenue. Explore galleries showcasing contemporary Turkish art, where local artists experiment with a fusion of tradition and innovation. Engage with gallery owners who passionately narrate the stories behind the artworks, turning your stroll into an art appreciation journey.

Fun Fact: A gallery curator once explained the symbolism behind a mural, providing a unique perspective on the intersection of modern art and cultural heritage.

Kadikoy: Evening Flavors at the Fish Market

As evening descends, cross the Bosphorus to Kadikoy, where the lively Fish Market awaits. Witness the transformation of the market as the lights come to life, creating a magical ambiance. Engage with fishmongers who skillfully prepare and grill the day's catch, offering a variety of seafood delights. Savor the evening flavors amidst the animated atmosphere of Kadikoy's culinary hotspot.

Insider Insight: A local chef once shared a secret spice blend for grilled fish, turning a casual chat into a culinary revelation.

Moda: Sunset Serenity on the Coast

Escape the bustle of the city and head to Moda for a tranquil sunset experience. Find a cozy spot along the Moda Coast, where locals gather to witness the sun dip below the horizon. Engage with residents who have made this daily ritual a part of their lives, capturing the serene beauty of the moment.

Anecdote Alert: A Moda local once spoke of the calming effect of the sunset, sharing how it became a source of inspiration for their daily reflections.

Fener & Balat: Nightfall Tales in Colorful Alleys

Venture into the historic neighborhoods of Fener and Balat as night falls, where the narrow alleys come alive with a kaleidoscope of colors. Explore the illuminated streets adorned with vibrant houses, street art, and eclectic shops. Engage with locals who share tales of the district's multicultural history, turning your night stroll into a journey through time.

Quirky Detail: A storyteller in Fener once recounted the humorous anecdotes of neighbors participating in an annual street decoration competition, bringing laughter to the neighborhood.

Uskudar: Midnight Serenade by the Maiden's Tower

Conclude your day in Uskudar, where the Maiden's Tower stands as a poetic sentinel in the moonlit waters. Experience a midnight serenade with the tower as your backdrop, surrounded by the gentle sounds of the Bosphorus. Engage with fellow night owls who appreciate the tranquility of the moment, creating a shared connection beneath the starry Istanbul sky.

Fun Fact: A local musician once played a traditional Turkish melody by the Maiden's Tower, adding a musical touch to the midnight ambiance.

As you bid adieu to the different neighborhoods of Istanbul, let the memories of each unique experience linger. From historical tales to artistic explorations and culinary delights, the daily rhythms of Istanbul's neighborhoods offer a vibrant mosaic that reflects the city's diverse and dynamic spirit.

10

HIDDEN HISTORIES

10.1 Forgotten Landmarks: Rediscovering Istanbul's Silent Narratives

Embark on a journey through the forgotten landmarks of Istanbul, where time has gently woven a tapestry of memories into the city's landscape. This guide invites you to peel back the layers of history, explore hidden gems, and uncover the silent narratives that echo through the streets. From neglected structures to overlooked corners, let's rediscover the charm of Istanbul's forgotten landmarks.

Envision this: You, stepping off the beaten path, the echoes of ancient whispers guiding your exploration, and the forgotten landmarks revealing tales that often escape the typical tourist's gaze. It's not just a guide; it's an invitation to unlock the secrets of Istanbul's overlooked treasures.

The Leaning Tower of Uskudar: A Quirky Asymmetry

In the heart of Uskudar stands a peculiar structure – the Leaning Tower. Not as famous as its counterpart in Pisa, this hidden gem tells a story of architectural eccentricity. Engage with locals who share anecdotes of the tower's unintentional tilt, offering a unique perspective on Uskudar's lesser-known landmarks.

Quirky Detail: Legend has it that the tower started leaning after a particularly lively celebration in the neighborhood, adding a touch of whimsy to its history.

Yedikule Dungeons: Shadows of the Past

Delve into the shadows of history at Yedikule Dungeons, a set of forgotten structures near the city walls. These underground chambers once housed prisoners during the Byzantine and Ottoman periods. Explore the eerie corridors, where the whispers of forgotten tales linger. Engage with guides who narrate stories of daring escapes and the resilience of those who faced imprisonment.

Anecdote Alert: A guide once shared a tale of a secret tunnel leading from the dungeons to the Sea of Marmara, sparking intrigue about the mysteries concealed beneath the city.

The Column of Constantine: A Silent Witness

Venture to the Column of Constantine, standing tall in the district of Fatih. Often overshadowed by the grandeur of nearby landmarks, this ancient column silently watches over the city. Engage with historians who reveal the significance of the column, from its Roman origins to its symbolic role in the Byzantine and Ottoman eras.

Fun Fact: Locals fondly refer to it as the 'Burnt Column' due to its slightly charred appearance, a result of a fire that swept through the city centuries ago.

Valens Aqueduct: An Aquatic Marvel

Trace the path of forgotten waterways at the Valens Aqueduct, an impressive structure that once supplied water to Constantinople. Wander beneath its arches and imagine the bustling life that once thrived around this engineering marvel. Engage with locals who share tales of the aqueduct's historical importance, from providing water for public baths to sustaining the daily lives of the city's residents.

Insider Insight: A resident once pointed out the strategic placement of the aqueduct, ensuring a continuous flow of water even during times of siege.

Theodosian Walls: Guardians of Byzantine Legacy

Step into the shadows of the Theodosian Walls, an expansive fortification that once protected Constantinople from invaders. Explore the well-preserved sections, each stone whispering stories of conquests, sieges, and the resilience of the city. Engage with archaeologists who unravel the architectural brilliance behind these ancient walls, revealing the secrets of their construction.

Quirky Detail: A local historian once recounted the tale of the "Kızkulesi Catapult," a creative solution to defend the city during times of conflict.

Laleli Complex: Ottoman Elegance Unveiled

Journey to Laleli Complex, tucked away in the Laleli district. This forgotten ensemble of Ottoman architecture houses a mosque, a theological school, and a library. Engage with preservationists who share stories of the complex's past glory, from its vibrant role in religious education to its serene courtyards adorned with tulip gardens.

Anecdote Alert: A preservationist once mentioned the intricate tilework in the mosque, revealing how each pattern tells a story about the craftsmen who adorned the walls.

As you rediscover Istanbul's forgotten landmarks, let the echoes of the past guide your exploration. These silent narratives, often overshadowed by more prominent attractions, add a layer of depth to the city's history, creating a mosaic of tales waiting to be unveiled by those who choose to venture off the well-trodden path.

10.2 Tales from the Past: Unveiling Istanbul's Historical Narratives

Embark on a captivating journey through the pages of history as we delve into the tales that linger in the nooks and crannies of Istanbul. This guide invites you to walk in the footsteps of emperors, poets, and everyday people whose stories have woven a rich tapestry that spans centuries. From palaces to hidden alleys, let's explore the tales that whisper through the stones of Istanbul.

Envision this: You, a time traveler in the heart of Istanbul, the echoes of bygone eras reverberating through the city, and the tales from the past coming to life with each step. It's not just a guide; it's an invitation to unearth the narratives that have shaped Istanbul's unique identity.

The Legend of Maiden's Tower: A Tale of Love and Isolation

Journey to the Maiden's Tower, where the waters of the Bosphorus cradle a legendary love story. Engage with storytellers who recount the tale of a king's daughter and the tragic fate that led to the tower's construction. Feel the romance in the air as you stand on the tower's terrace, gazing at the city lights that twinkle like distant stars.

Anecdote Alert: A local guide once shared a whimsical version of the tale, adding a touch of humor to the centuries-old love story.

Gallipoli: Echoes of Valor and Sacrifice

Venture beyond the city limits to Gallipoli, where the echoes of World War I resonate. Explore the battlefields and memorials that stand as silent witnesses to the valor and sacrifice of soldiers from different nations. Engage with historians who share poignant anecdotes about the resilience of those who fought and the bonds forged in the crucible of war.

Quirky Detail: A descendant of a Gallipoli soldier once shared a heartfelt letter penned by their ancestor, providing a personal perspective on the wartime experience.

The Grand Bazaar: Merchants of Time

Step into the bustling labyrinth of the Grand Bazaar, where the air is thick with the scent of spices and the vibrant hues of textiles. Engage with seasoned merchants who share tales of the bazaar's evolution through the ages. Discover the secrets behind age-old crafts, from carpet weaving to intricate metalwork, as artisans unveil the history woven into their creations.

Insider Insight: A master carpet weaver once revealed the symbolism hidden in the patterns, turning a simple rug into a canvas of cultural expression.

Suleymaniye Mosque: Architectural Splendor and Imperial Dreams

Enter the Suleymaniye Mosque, a masterpiece of Ottoman architecture that whispers tales of imperial ambition. Engage with guides who unravel the architectural symbolism and the dreams of Suleiman the Magnificent that inspired its construction. Stand in awe beneath the majestic dome, envisioning the prayers and ceremonies that have echoed through its sacred halls.

Fun Fact: A local historian once highlighted the unique acoustics of the mosque, where a single whisper can be heard clearly throughout the vast interior.

Istanbul's Spice Bazaar: A Culinary Tapestry

Wander through the Spice Bazaar, where the aromatic symphony of spices has unfolded for centuries. Engage with spice merchants who share stories of the bazaar's role in ancient trade routes. Taste the flavors of exotic spices and savor Turkish delights as you become a part of the culinary tapestry that has enchanted palates throughout history.

Quirky Detail: A spice vendor once demonstrated the art of creating the perfect Turkish coffee blend, imparting the wisdom passed down through generations.

Balat's Colorful Streets: Chronicles of Diversity

Immerse yourself in the kaleidoscopic streets of Balat, where centuries of cultural diversity have left their mark. Engage with residents who share stories of the district's transformation from a hub of Jewish life to a vibrant mosaic of cultures. Witness the colors of Balat's houses, each shade telling a tale of its own, reflecting the resilient spirit of the community.

Anecdote Alert: A local artist once shared the inspiration behind the vibrant murals that adorn Balat's streets, adding a contemporary layer to its historical narrative.

As you uncover these tales from the past, let the city of Istanbul become a living chronicle, where the stories of empires, heroes, and ordinary people merge to create a narrative that transcends time. Each cobblestone and archway becomes a page turned, inviting you to explore the depth and richness of Istanbul's historical tapestry.

10.3 Unexplored Corners: Istanbul's Hidden Gems Beckon

Embark on a quest to discover the enchanting secrets concealed within Istanbul's unexplored corners. This guide invites you to wander off the beaten path, where lesser-known treasures await your exploration. From tucked-away neighborhoods to obscure alleys, let's unveil the magic that lies beyond the bustling thoroughfares of Istanbul.

Picture this: You, a modern-day explorer, navigating the labyrinth of Istanbul's hidden corners, each step revealing a new facet of the city's charm. It's not just a guide; it's an invitation to unravel the mysteries that adorn the less-explored tapestry of Istanbul.

Fener & Balat: A Tapestry of Colors and Cultures

Begin your journey in Fener and Balat, two neighborhoods that have preserved Istanbul's multicultural heritage. Wander through narrow alleys adorned with vibrant houses, where Greek, Armenian, and Ottoman influences blend seamlessly. Engage with locals who share stories of communal harmony and the centuries-old traditions that define these colorful neighborhoods.

Anecdote Alert: A resident once recounted the annual "Fener-Balat Festival," where residents celebrate the district's cultural diversity with music, dance, and shared meals.

Kuzguncuk: A Tranquil Bosphorus Retreat

Escape the bustling city to discover the serene charm of Kuzguncuk, a hidden gem nestled along the Bosphorus. Stroll through peaceful streets lined with Ottoman-era houses, explore quaint shops, and enjoy a cup of Turkish tea at a waterside café. Engage with locals who appreciate the tranquility of Kuzguncuk and proudly share their favorite spots.

Quirky Detail: A Kuzguncuk regular once pointed out a centuries-old tree in the neighborhood, believed to have witnessed the rise and fall of empires.

Yildiz Porcelain Factory: Artistry Preserved in Time

Step back in time at the Yildiz Porcelain Factory, a lesser-known gem that echoes Istanbul's artistic history. Explore the workshops where skilled artisans continue the age-old tradition of crafting exquisite porcelain. Engage with craftsmen who share stories of the factory's royal commissions and its role in preserving Turkish artistic heritage.

Fun Fact: A porcelain artist once demonstrated the delicate process of hand-painting intricate patterns, highlighting the dedication required for each unique piece.

Beykoz: The Hillside Haven

Ascend the hills of Beykoz, a district that offers panoramic views of the Bosphorus. Wander through vineyards, visit Ottoman-era mansions, and indulge in the tranquility that defines this hillside haven. Engage with locals who share stories of Beykoz's transformation from a rural retreat to a charming enclave, offering a perfect escape from the urban hustle.

Insider Insight: A Beykoz resident once recommended a secluded spot for watching the sunrise over the Bosphorus, turning a simple morning stroll into a poetic experience.

Balik Pazari: Culinary Treasures Beyond the Grand Bazaar

Discover Balik Pazari, a hidden culinary gem that stands in the shadows of the Grand Bazaar. Dive into a bustling market where locals gather for the freshest seafood and aromatic spices. Engage with fishermen who proudly display their catch of the day, sharing insights into Istanbul's culinary traditions and the importance of sustainable fishing practices.

Anecdote Alert: A fishmonger once shared a family recipe for preparing the perfect seafood meze, turning a market visit into a gastronomic adventure.

Emirgan Park: A Blossoming Retreat

Conclude your exploration in Emirgan Park, an oasis of greenery and blooms along the Bosphorus. Wander through manicured gardens, enjoy a leisurely boat ride, and marvel at the historic pavilions that grace the park. Engage with park enthusiasts who reveal the seasonal transformations, from tulip festivals in spring to the vibrant hues of autumn.

Quirky Detail: A park regular once shared a tip for capturing the most enchanting photos of the tulip beds, turning a casual stroll into a photographic adventure.

As you venture into Istanbul's unexplored corners, let the city unveil its hidden treasures, each corner a testament to the rich tapestry of history, culture, and nature that defines this captivating metropolis.

10.4 Mysteries and Legends: Istanbul's Enigmatic Tapestry

Embark on a journey into the mystical and legendary side of Istanbul, where tales of the supernatural, ancient mysteries, and mythical beings intertwine with the city's history. This guide invites you to unravel the enigmatic threads that weave through the streets, revealing the hidden stories that add a layer of intrigue to Istanbul's captivating narrative.

Imagine this: You, a seeker of the unknown, delving into the mysteries that shroud Istanbul's past, where whispers of legends and untold stories linger in the air. It's not just a guide; it's an invitation to step into the realm of the mystical and explore the secrets that time has concealed.

The Ghosts of Pera Palace: Haunting Elegance

Begin your exploration at the Pera Palace Hotel, an elegant establishment with a storied history. Engage with staff members who share tales of mysterious occurrences, from unexplained sounds to sightings of spectral figures. Feel the echoes of the past as you walk through the hotel's corridors, where the presence of famous guests and enigmatic events lingers.

Anecdote Alert: A hotel employee once recounted an encounter with a guest who claimed to have glimpsed a woman in vintage attire, adding an element of eerie fascination to the Pera Palace's allure.

Basilica Cistern: Subterranean Secrets

Descend into the Basilica Cistern, a vast underground chamber that conceals more than meets the eye. Explore the dimly lit pathways surrounded by ancient columns and listen to the echoes of dripping water. Engage with guides who reveal the mysterious Medusa heads hidden among the columns, sparking curiosity about the cistern's secretive past.

Quirky Detail: A guide once shared a local belief that the upside-down Medusa head was placed intentionally to neutralize the gaze of the mythical creature.

The Legend of Rumeli Hisari: Maiden's Tower's Silent Guardian

Venture to Rumeli Hisari, a fortress guarding the Bosphorus. Engage with historians who share tales of the construction's speed, rumored to have been achieved through supernatural means. Explore the battlements where legends of a jinn, a mythical being, assisting in the construction add an air of mystery to this strategically placed fortress.

Fun Fact: A local storyteller once recounted a folk tale of the jinn, claiming that those who listen closely might still hear its whispers on quiet nights.

Kucuksu Pavilion: Imperial Intrigues

Visit the Kucuksu Pavilion, a waterside retreat with a history shrouded in imperial intrigues. Engage with guides who narrate stories of secret rendezvous, whispered conversations, and the clandestine affairs of Ottoman royalty. Stroll through the pavilion's rooms, where echoes of the past intertwine with the tranquil beauty of the Bosphorus.

Insider Insight: A guide once shared an anecdote about a hidden passage believed to connect the pavilion to a nearby palace, adding a layer of mystery to the site.

Gulhane Park: The Enchanted Grove

Explore Gulhane Park, a lush expanse that conceals tales of enchanted groves and magical gardens. Engage with park enthusiasts who share stories of historical events and legendary creatures said to have frequented the park. Wander beneath ancient trees and discover the hidden corners where the park's mystical aura comes to life.

Anecdote Alert: A regular visitor once shared a whimsical story about encountering a wise old cat that seemed to understand the park's secrets.

Galata Tower: Whispers from the Heights

Ascend the Galata Tower, where panoramic views of Istanbul unfold. Engage with guides who share legends of mystical creatures that once roamed the streets below. Feel the breeze at the tower's summit and listen for whispers carried by the wind, adding a touch of magic to the cityscape.

Quirky Detail: A guide once playfully pointed out a spot on the tower's terrace, claiming it as the perfect vantage point for glimpsing mythical beings.

As you unravel the mysteries and legends woven into Istanbul's fabric, let the city's mystical side captivate your imagination. Each site, with its tales of ghosts, jinn, and hidden passages, adds a layer of enchantment to the historical tapestry that is Istanbul.

11

PRACTICAL TIPS FOR TRAVELERS

11.1 Iconic Photo Spots: Framing Istanbul's Timeless Beauty

Embark on a visual journey through Istanbul's most picturesque locations, where every corner becomes a canvas for capturing the city's timeless charm. This guide invites you to explore the iconic photo spots that promise not just snapshots but memories etched in pixels. From historic landmarks to hidden gems, let's discover the frames that encapsulate Istanbul's enchanting allure.

Visualize this: You, a photographer capturing the essence of Istanbul, framing moments that transcend the ordinary. It's not just a guide; it's an invitation to turn your lens towards the beauty that awaits at every turn in this mesmerizing city.

The Blue Mosque: A Skyline Symphony

Begin your photographic odyssey at the Blue Mosque, where six minarets pierce the sky like elegant spires. Find the perfect angle to capture the mosque's domes against the vibrant hues of the Istanbul sky. Engage with locals who share anecdotes about the mosque's architectural splendor, guiding you to unveil its beauty through your lens.

Anecdote Alert: A seasoned photographer once mentioned the magic of capturing the Blue Mosque at sunrise when the soft light bathes its intricate details, creating a celestial atmosphere.

Hagia Sophia: Timeless Elegance in Stone

Move to Hagia Sophia, an architectural masterpiece that tells tales of empires and conversions. Explore the exterior, framing its grandeur against the modern city backdrop. Engage with fellow photographers who share tips on capturing the interplay of light and shadow on the centuries-old walls, adding depth to your visual storytelling.

Quirky Detail: A photography enthusiast once revealed a hidden courtyard offering a unique perspective of Hagia Sophia, showcasing its majestic domes in a more intimate setting.

Bosphorus Strait: A Waterfront Tapestry

Stroll along the Bosphorus Strait, where the cityscape meets the tranquil waters. Capture the contrast of historic palaces against modern developments, framed by the natural beauty of the strait. Engage with boatmen who share stories about the changing skyline and guide you to the best spots for photographing Istanbul's waterfront charm.

Insider Insight: A local photographer once recommended capturing the Bosphorus at twilight, when the city lights dance on the water, creating a mesmerizing spectacle.

Sultanahmet Square: History in Every Frame

Explore Sultanahmet Square, a historical hub surrounded by architectural marvels. Frame the square's vastness, encompassing the Obelisk of Theodosius and the German Fountain. Engage with locals who appreciate the square's significance and share tips on capturing the dynamic energy of events that often unfold in this central space.

Fun Fact: A street photographer once shared stories of chance encounters and serendipitous moments captured in Sultanahmet Square, emphasizing the importance of being ready for the unexpected.

Galata Bridge: Bridges and Silhouettes

Head to Galata Bridge, where the city's energy converges. Frame the bridge's iconic silhouette against the backdrop of the Golden Horn. Engage with anglers who frequent the bridge and add a human element to your shots. Capture the bustling life on the bridge, where fishermen share stories and locals pass by in a captivating dance of urban rhythm.

Anecdote Alert: A street artist once described the bridge as a stage where everyday stories unfold, providing endless opportunities for candid shots.

Sunset at Ortakoy Mosque: A Golden Hour Gem

Conclude your photographic journey at Ortakoy Mosque, where the Bosphorus sparkles with the hues of the setting sun. Frame the mosque against the twilight sky, capturing the magical transition from day to night. Engage with fellow photographers who gather to witness this daily spectacle and share insights on capturing the play of light during Istanbul's golden hour.

Quirky Detail: A local storyteller once mentioned the tradition of sipping tea at waterfront cafes while waiting for the perfect sunset shot, turning the experience into a shared ritual among photographers.

As you navigate Istanbul's iconic photo spots, let each frame tell a story, preserving not just the visuals but the emotions and narratives that make this city truly unique. Whether you're an aspiring photographer or a casual snap-happy explorer, Istanbul's beauty is ready to be immortalized through your lens.

11.2 Capturing Local Life: Istanbul's Everyday Tapestry

Embark on a photographic exploration of Istanbul's vibrant streets, where the pulse of local life beats in harmony with the city's timeless spirit. This guide invites you to step beyond the postcard views and capture the candid moments that define Istanbul's everyday rhythm. From bustling markets to quiet neighborhoods, let's frame the stories of the people who bring this metropolis to life.

Visualize this: You, a storyteller through the lens, documenting the nuances of daily life in Istanbul, where every face and every corner becomes a chapter in the city's living story. It's not just a guide; it's an invitation to be a part of the scenes that unfold in Istanbul's everyday tapestry.

Grand Bazaar: Merchants and Mosaics

Begin your exploration at the Grand Bazaar, a bustling labyrinth where shopkeepers beckon with vibrant displays. Frame the artisans at work, their hands weaving intricate patterns into carpets or crafting delicate jewelry. Engage with merchants who share anecdotes about the market's centuries-old history and the artistry that defines their trade.

Anecdote Alert: A rug seller once narrated the story behind a centuries-old carpet, passed down through generations, turning a mere transaction into a glimpse into familial traditions.

Balik Pazari: The Pulse of Culinary Life

Wander through Balik Pazari, the lively fish market, where the catch of the day takes center stage. Frame the animated exchanges between vendors and customers, capturing the vibrant colors and textures of the seafood on display. Engage with fishermen who share their daily routines, offering a glimpse into the sustainable fishing practices that have sustained Istanbul's culinary traditions.

Quirky Detail: A fishmonger once shared a playful rivalry with a neighboring stall, adding a touch of camaraderie to the competitive atmosphere of the market.

Street Art in Karakoy: Walls that Speak

Explore the streets of Karakoy, a district adorned with vibrant street art that tells stories of rebellion and cultural expression. Frame the graffiti that adorns the walls, capturing the ever-evolving urban canvas. Engage with local artists who share insights into the messages behind their creations, turning the streets into a visual dialogue between the city and its inhabitants.

Insider Insight: A street artist once revealed the collaborative nature of the local art scene, where murals are often created through collective efforts and shared visions.

Tea Gardens in Uskudar: Conversations Over Cay

Capture the essence of social life at the tea gardens in Uskudar, where locals gather to share conversations over glasses of Turkish tea. Frame the animated discussions, the clinking of glasses, and the steam rising from the traditional tea pots. Engage with patrons who discuss everything from daily happenings to philosophical musings, offering a window into the communal nature of Istanbul's social spaces.

Fun Fact: A tea garden regular once mentioned a silent pact among patrons to maintain a tranquil atmosphere, turning the space into a haven for contemplation.

Kadikoy Market: A Melody of Colors

Immerse yourself in the kaleidoscopic atmosphere of Kadikoy Market, where fresh produce and spices create a symphony of colors. Frame the interactions between vendors and customers, capturing the lively exchanges and the eclectic array of goods on display. Engage with sellers who share stories about sourcing their produce locally, emphasizing the importance of community connections.

Anecdote Alert: A fruit vendor once recounted the challenges of predicting Istanbul's unpredictable weather and its impact on crop yields, offering a glimpse into the intricacies of the local supply chain.

Children Playing in Gulhane Park: Innocence Preserved

Conclude your photographic journey at Gulhane Park, a haven of greenery where children play freely. Frame the laughter, the energy, and the timeless innocence of youth against the backdrop of historical landmarks. Engage with families who share the significance of the park in their daily lives, turning your lens towards moments that transcend generations.

Quirky Detail: A parent once shared a humorous anecdote about their child's imaginative play in the park, turning a routine day into a memorable family story.

As you capture the essence of local life in Istanbul, let each photograph become a window into the vibrant, diverse, and ever-evolving tapestry of the city. Through your lens, document the stories that unfold in the streets, markets, and parks, preserving the authenticity that makes Istanbul a living, breathing mosaic of cultures and communities.

11.3 Night Photography: Istanbul's Nocturnal Symphony

Embark on a visual odyssey as the sun sets over Istanbul, and the city transforms into a mesmerizing canvas of lights and shadows. This guide invites you to capture the magic of Istanbul after dark, where ancient landmarks, bustling streets, and the Bosphorus come alive in a nocturnal symphony. From the glow of minarets to the reflections on the water, let's unveil the secrets of Istanbul's night through your lens.

Visualize this: You, a nocturnal storyteller, navigating the city's illuminated landscapes, where each frame encapsulates the enchantment of Istanbul under the moonlit sky. It's not just a guide; it's an invitation to explore the after-hours allure that transforms Istanbul into a breathtaking spectacle.

Blue Mosque Illuminations: Moonlit Elegance

Begin your night photography escapade at the Blue Mosque, where the minarets and domes are bathed in a soft, celestial glow. Frame the intricate details against the night sky, capturing the play of light on the centuries-old architecture. Engage with locals who appreciate the mosque's ethereal beauty at night and share tips on finding the perfect angle.

Anecdote Alert: A night guard once shared the serenity that envelops the mosque after hours, turning the Blue Mosque into a haven for contemplation.

Galata Tower: A Beacon in the Night

Ascend the Galata Tower as the city lights begin to twinkle below. Frame the tower against the city's nocturnal panorama, capturing the blend of historical grandeur and modern vibrancy. Engage with fellow night photographers who share their favorite moments at the tower, from citywide fireworks to the tranquil moments when the streets below are hushed.

Quirky Detail: A rooftop enthusiast once revealed a secret vantage point near the tower, offering a unique perspective of the city lights and the tower's silhouette.

Bosphorus Cruise: Lights on the Water

Embark on a nighttime Bosphorus cruise, where the city's reflections dance on the water's surface. Frame the illuminated shores, capturing the interplay of lights from historical palaces to modern waterfront developments. Engage with boat captains who navigate the Bosphorus every night, providing insights into the best routes for capturing Istanbul's skyline from the water.

Insider Insight: A seasoned photographer once recommended a slow cruise during the twilight hours, capturing the transition from sunset to the city's sparkling nocturnal ambiance.

Istiklal Avenue: Neon Trails and City Buzz

Stroll down Istiklal Avenue, where neon signs and bustling crowds create a lively nocturnal ambiance. Frame the avenue's dynamic energy, capturing the streaks of light left by passing trams and the vibrant storefronts. Engage with locals who frequent Istiklal Avenue after dark, sharing stories of impromptu street performances and the eclectic mix of nightlife that defines this central artery.

Fun Fact: A street musician once shared the spontaneity of Istiklal Avenue, where impromptu jam sessions often create memorable moments for both performers and passersby.

Suleymaniye Mosque: Silhouetted Grandeur

Capture the silhouette of the Suleymaniye Mosque against the night sky, its majestic domes and minarets outlined by subtle lighting. Frame the mosque from various angles, experimenting with the interplay of shadows and lights. Engage with night photographers who frequent the mosque, sharing tips on long-exposure techniques to enhance the ethereal quality of the nighttime scene.

Anecdote Alert: A photography enthusiast once recounted capturing a meteor shower above the Suleymaniye Mosque, turning a routine night shoot into a celestial spectacle.

Karakoy and Golden Horn: Harbor Lights

Conclude your night photography adventure at Karakoy and the Golden Horn, where harbor lights shimmer on the water's surface. Frame the reflections of illuminated buildings, capturing the magical ambiance of Istanbul's waterfront. Engage with locals who appreciate the romance of the Golden Horn at night and share anecdotes about moonlit walks along the shores.

Quirky Detail: A dockworker once shared the rhythmic beauty of the harbor at night, where the sounds of lapping waves and distant ship horns create a unique nocturnal soundtrack.

As you navigate Istanbul's nocturnal symphony, let your camera be the conductor, capturing the city's after-hours allure with every click. From iconic landmarks to hidden corners, let the night reveal Istanbul in a new, enchanting light, turning your photographs into a visual love letter to the city that never sleeps.

11.4 Seasonal Visual Delights: Istanbul's Ever-Changing Canvas

Embark on a journey through the seasons in Istanbul, where the city's landscapes undergo a magical transformation, offering a visual feast for those eager to capture its ever-changing beauty. This guide invites you to synchronize your lens with the rhythm of nature, exploring how each season adds its unique brushstroke to Istanbul's canvas. From the vibrant hues of spring to the cozy winter charm, let's discover the seasonal visual delights that make Istanbul a year-round spectacle.

Visualize this: You, a seasonal observer, capturing the kaleidoscope of Istanbul's beauty as it transitions through the months, weaving a tale of nature's influence on this ancient metropolis. It's not just a guide; it's an invitation to explore the diverse moods and colors that paint Istanbul in every season.

Spring Blossoms: Tulip Time Extravaganza

Welcome spring in Istanbul, where millions of tulips bloom in a riot of colors across parks, gardens, and city squares. Frame the vibrant tulip carpets against the backdrop of historic landmarks, capturing the essence of Istanbul's springtime. Engage with locals who eagerly anticipate the annual Tulip Festival, sharing anecdotes about the symbolism of tulips in Turkish culture.

Anecdote Alert: A tulip enthusiast once shared the joy of discovering rare tulip varieties in unexpected corners of the city, turning a casual stroll into a botanical adventure.

Summer Serenity: Bosphorus Breezes and Rooftop Sunsets

Embrace the warmth of summer as the Bosphorus becomes a playground of shimmering reflections and gentle breezes. Frame the sunset from Istanbul's rooftops, capturing the city bathed in the golden hues of the evening sun. Engage with locals who savor rooftop moments during summer, sharing stories about their favorite spots for witnessing the magical transition from day to night.

Quirky Detail: A rooftop regular once recommended sipping a cool beverage while watching the seagulls dance in the sky during summer sunsets, adding a touch of poetic charm to the experience.

Autumnal Mosaic: Golden Foliage in Parks and Palaces

Witness Istanbul's parks and historic palaces transform into a golden mosaic as autumn sets in. Frame the rust-colored leaves against the timeless architecture, capturing the juxtaposition of nature's changing palette with the city's enduring landmarks. Engage with park-goers who appreciate the tranquility of autumn in Istanbul, sharing tips on finding the hidden corners where fall's beauty shines.

Insider Insight: A local artist once described the mesmerizing effect of autumn's golden hour on the city's stone facades, creating a warm, nostalgic atmosphere.

Winter Whispers: Cozy Streets and Festive Lights

Experience the coziness of winter in Istanbul, where streets adorned with festive lights and seasonal decorations create a warm ambiance. Frame the city's iconic landmarks against the winter night, capturing the reflections on wet cobblestones. Engage with locals who relish winter strolls, sharing anecdotes about spontaneous snowball fights and impromptu gatherings in cozy cafes.

Fun Fact: A café owner once shared the tradition of serving hot sahlep, a comforting winter drink, to customers seeking refuge from the cold, turning a simple beverage into a seasonal ritual.

Foggy Mystique: Bosphorus in Winter Veils

Capture the Bosphorus as winter brings a touch of mystery, veiling the cityscape in ethereal fog. Frame the silhouettes of boats and waterfront structures emerging from the mist, creating an enchanting visual spectacle. Engage with boat captains who navigate the foggy waters, sharing insights into the unique challenges and beauty of winter cruises.

Anecdote Alert: A captain once recounted navigating through the Bosphorus fog, describing the sensation of being surrounded by a sea of tranquility with only distant echoes.

Festive Markets: Seasonal Bustle and Cheer

Explore Istanbul's festive markets as winter holidays approach, where stalls brim with seasonal treats and handmade crafts. Frame the market scenes, capturing the joyous atmosphere and the smiles of both vendors and visitors. Engage with market-goers who share stories of cherished traditions, turning these bustling markets into a cultural snapshot of seasonal celebrations.

Quirky Detail: A vendor once shared the popularity of handmade ornaments crafted from recycled materials, adding an eco-friendly twist to the festive market experience.

As you navigate Istanbul's ever-changing seasons, let your camera be the storyteller, capturing the city's natural and cultural evolution with each passing month. From the blooming tulips of spring to the festive cheer of winter, let your photographs become a visual journey through the diverse and enchanting tapestry of Istanbul's yearly cycle.

12

PRACTICAL TIPS FOR TRAVELERS

12.1 Language Tips: Unlocking the Melody of Turkish Communication

Embark on a linguistic adventure in Istanbul, where the cadence of Turkish language intertwines with the city's rich cultural tapestry. This guide invites you to not just learn phrases but to embrace the poetic dance of words that shape everyday interactions. From essential expressions to the beauty of Turkish script, let's unravel the secrets of effective communication, fostering connections that go beyond words.

Visualize this: You, a linguistic explorer, navigating the sounds of Turkish, turning every interaction into a lyrical exchange. It's not just a guide; it's an invitation to immerse yourself in the heartbeat of Istanbul's language, where every word becomes a brushstroke on the canvas of cultural understanding.

Essential Greetings: Embracing the Turkish Hello

Begin your language journey with the art of greetings, where a simple "Merhaba" (Hello) unlocks doors to warm interactions. Frame your introduction with a genuine smile, capturing the universal language of friendliness. Engage with locals who appreciate a well-pronounced "Merhaba," sharing stories of how a warm greeting sets the tone for positive encounters.

Anecdote Alert: A traveler once shared the transformative power of a sincere "Merhaba" in a small teahouse, turning strangers into companions eager to share tales of the city.

Navigating Politeness: The Art of "Lütfen" and "Teşekkür Ederim"

Explore the nuances of politeness with "Lütfen" (Please) and "Teşekkür Ederim" (Thank you). Frame your requests and expressions of gratitude with these phrases, adding a touch of courtesy to your interactions. Engage with locals who appreciate the effort to incorporate these words, sharing anecdotes about the cultural significance of polite exchanges.

Quirky Detail: A café owner once remarked on the joy of hearing "Lütfen" and "Teşekkür Ederim" from visitors, creating a harmonious atmosphere in the establishment.

Mastering Basic Numbers: The Currency of Communication

Dive into the numerical rhythm of Turkish by mastering basic numbers. Frame your transactions with confidence, whether bargaining in the Grand Bazaar or ordering a delicious kebab. Engage with shopkeepers who share stories of travelers mastering numbers with ease, turning simple transactions into delightful cross-cultural experiences.

Insider Insight: A seasoned traveler once shared the liberating feeling of negotiating prices in Turkish, transforming mundane exchanges into moments of shared laughter.

Getting Directions: Navigating Istanbul's Labyrinth

Conquer the art of asking for directions with phrases like "Nerede?" (Where is?) and "Sağa/Sola"

(Right/Left). Frame your inquiries with a friendly demeanor, capturing the willingness of locals to guide you through the city's labyrinthine streets. Engage with pedestrians who share stories of tourists turning lost moments into opportunities for spontaneous exploration.

Fun Fact: A local once recalled a delightful encounter with a lost traveler, turning a simple direction-giving session into an impromptu neighborhood tour.

Embracing Turkish Script: Calligraphy in Communication

Immerse yourself in the aesthetic beauty of Turkish script, a poetic dance of curves and dots. Frame your fascination with the elegance of "Osmanlıca" (Ottoman Turkish) and modern Turkish script, capturing the visual allure of this written art form. Engage with calligraphy enthusiasts who share anecdotes about the script's historical significance and evolving styles.

Anecdote Alert: An artist once shared the meditative quality of practicing calligraphy, turning the act of writing into a journey of self-expression and cultural connection.

Local Slang and Expressions: Adding Flavor to Conversations

Elevate your language skills with a sprinkle of local slang and expressions. Frame your conversations with phrases like "Vay be!" (Wow!) and "Tamam" (Okay), capturing the vibrancy of colloquial Turkish. Engage with locals who appreciate the lighthearted use of slang, sharing humorous anecdotes that showcase the dynamic nature of language.

Quirky Detail: A language enthusiast once recounted the joy of seamlessly incorporating local expressions, turning casual chats into moments of shared laughter with newfound friends.

As you delve into the melody of Turkish communication, let each phrase become a brushstroke, painting a canvas of cross-cultural connections. Whether you're bargaining in the bazaars or savoring tea in a local café, let the language of Istanbul be your guide, creating a symphony of understanding that transcends words.

12.2 Safety Guidelines: Navigating Istanbul Securely

Welcome to Istanbul, a city pulsating with life and culture. Ensuring your safety is our priority, and this guide provides essential safety guidelines to make your exploration of this enchanting city not only memorable but also secure. From navigating bustling markets to strolling through historic neighborhoods, these guidelines are your compass to a worry-free experience.

Visualize this: You, a confident explorer, navigating Istanbul's vibrant streets with an awareness that blends seamlessly into your journey. It's not just a guide; it's your safety companion, ensuring that every step you take is both adventurous and secure.

City Awareness: Your First Line of Defense

Stay Informed: Familiarize yourself with the local emergency services, nearest hospitals, and your embassy's contact information. This knowledge ensures quick access to assistance if needed.

Local Contacts: Keep a list of local contacts, including your accommodation, local friends, or guides. It's always handy to have someone familiar with the city to call upon.

Public Transportation Safety: Moving Around with Confidence

Secure Valuables: While using public transportation, keep your belongings secure. Be mindful of crowded areas, and consider using anti-theft accessories such as money belts and secure backpacks.

Validate Transportation: When using taxis or rideshares, ensure they are official and use registered services. Confirm the fare before starting your journey.

Street Smarts: Navigating Busy Areas

Blend In: Dress like a local to avoid standing out as a tourist. This can help deter pickpockets and make your exploration more discreet.

Maps and Navigation: Use digital maps or have a physical map handy. This not only helps you navigate but also avoids drawing unnecessary attention to yourself.

Health and Wellness: Prioritizing Your Well-being

Hydration: Istanbul's climate can be diverse. Stay hydrated, especially during warmer months, to ensure your well-being.

Medical Precautions: If you have specific health concerns or require medication, carry a small medical kit and a list of essential contacts, including your doctor's information.

Cultural Respect: Fostering Positive Interactions

Respect Local Customs: Familiarize yourself with local customs and traditions to ensure respectful interactions. This cultural awareness enhances your experience and contributes to a harmonious stay.

Language Basics: Learn a few basic phrases in Turkish. This not only facilitates communication but also demonstrates your interest in local culture.

Nighttime Exploration: Enjoying Istanbul's Nightlife Safely

Group Safety: When exploring nightlife, especially in unfamiliar areas, stick to well-lit and populated places. Going out in groups enhances both enjoyment and safety.

Transportation Arrangements: Plan your return transportation in advance, especially if you'll be out late. Avoid unregistered taxis and opt for reputable services.

Emergency Preparedness: Knowing What to Do

Emergency Numbers: Memorize or save local emergency numbers, including police, medical services, and your country's embassy or consulate.

Communication Plan: Establish a communication plan with travel companions, especially if you're exploring separately. Share your itinerary and check in regularly.

These safety guidelines are designed to empower you to explore Istanbul confidently. While the city invites you to immerse yourself in its beauty, culture, and history, following these guidelines ensures that your journey is not only enriching but also secure. Istanbul awaits – embrace it safely and make lasting memories!

12.3 Internet and Connectivity: Navigating Istanbul in the Digital Age

In the heart of Istanbul, where the past meets the present, staying connected is a key to unlocking the city's wonders. This guide on internet and connectivity ensures that you not only explore the enchanting streets but also seamlessly navigate the digital landscape. From sharing your Turkish adventures on social media to finding your way through the city, these tips will keep you connected and informed.

Visualize this: You, a modern-day explorer, capturing the essence of Istanbul both in your memories and in the digital realm. It's not just a guide; it's your passport to staying online, sharing your experiences, and making the most of Istanbul's digital tapestry.

Local SIM Cards: Your Gateway to Seamless Connectivity

Purchase a Local SIM Card: Visit one of Istanbul's numerous mobile operators to grab a local SIM card. This provides you with a local phone number and data, ensuring affordable connectivity during your stay.

Top-Up Options: Easily top up your mobile data and minutes at kiosks, convenience stores, or through mobile apps offered by local providers. It's a hassle-free way to stay connected.

Public Wi-Fi: Connecting on the Go

Wi-Fi Availability: Istanbul boasts an extensive network of free Wi-Fi hotspots in cafes, restaurants, public spaces, and even public transportation. Look for the "Wi-Fi" signs to connect effortlessly.

Secure Connections: When using public Wi-Fi, prioritize secure connections, especially for activities that involve personal information. Consider using a virtual private network (VPN) for added security.

Internet Cafés: A Digital Oasis

Internet Cafés: For a dedicated online session or if you don't have a personal device, Istanbul has a variety of internet cafés where you can check emails, update social media, or simply browse the web.

Navigational Apps: Your Digital Compass in the City

Digital Maps: Leverage navigation apps like Google Maps, Yandex Maps, or local alternatives to navigate Istanbul's intricate streets. These apps offer real-time updates on traffic, public transportation, and walking routes.

Language Translation Apps: Break language barriers with translation apps like Google Translate. They're invaluable for communicating in Turkish and understanding local signage.

Mobile Payment: Embracing Cashless Convenience

Digital Wallets: Many establishments in Istanbul accept mobile payments. Link your credit card or use local digital wallets for a seamless and secure cashless experience.

Online Safety: A Digital Shield

Secure Your Devices: Keep your devices protected with passwords and update your software regularly to enhance security.

Data Roaming: If you plan to use data roaming, check with your home provider for international plans to avoid unexpected charges.

Social Media Sharing: Documenting Your Journey

Capture and Share: Share your Istanbul adventures on social media platforms. Capture the beauty of the city and connect with fellow travelers using popular hashtags.

Local Apps: Explore local apps that provide insights into Istanbul's cultural events, dining recommendations, and real-time updates on city life.

Staying connected in Istanbul enhances your travel experience, whether you're navigating historic sites, sharing your favorite Turkish dish on Instagram, or finding your way through the city's labyrinthine streets. Embrace the digital era in this ancient metropolis, where connectivity enriches your journey and makes Istanbul truly feel like home.

13

APPENDIX

13.1 Useful Phrases: Your Key to Seamless Conversations in Istanbul

Embark on a linguistic journey through Istanbul armed with a toolkit of indispensable phrases that will open doors to genuine connections and smooth interactions. This guide isn't just a list of words; it's a passport to cultural understanding and a gateway to the heart of this vibrant city. From basic greetings to expressing gratitude, let's explore the phrases that will make your Istanbul experience truly unforgettable.

Visualize this: You, a linguistic maestro, effortlessly navigating the streets of Istanbul with phrases that resonate with the locals. It's not just a guide; it's an invitation to immerse yourself in the richness of the Turkish language, transforming every conversation into a shared moment of connection.

Essential Greetings: Setting the Tone

Merhaba! (mehr-HAH-bah) - Hello!

Frame this phrase with a warm smile, and you'll find yourself welcomed into the heart of Istanbul's hospitality.

Günaydın! (goo-NIGH-dun) - Good morning!

Perfect for starting your day with a friendly greeting, whether at a local cafe or the bustling markets.

İyi akşamlar! (ee-yee ahk-shahm-LAHR) - Good evening!

As the day transitions, use this phrase to greet locals and fellow wanderers alike.

Politeness Matters: Expressing Gratitude

Teşekkür ederim. (teh-shehk-KOOR ed-AIR-im) - Thank you.

A simple phrase that goes a long way; use it to express appreciation in shops, restaurants, or when someone lends a helping hand.

Lütfen. (LOOT-fen) - Please.

Add this to your requests for a touch of politeness, whether you're ordering a meal or seeking assistance.

Navigating Conversations: Seeking Information

Nerede? (Ner-eh-deh) - Where is...?

Useful for getting directions, locating landmarks, or finding that hidden gem you've heard about.

Kaç para? (Kahch PAH-rah) - How much is it?

Essential for navigating the Grand Bazaar or negotiating prices in local markets.

Common Courtesies: Making Connections

Evet. (EH-vet) - Yes.

A simple affirmation to show agreement or consent in various situations.

Hayır. (HAH-yuhr) - No.

A polite way to decline or express disagreement.

Survival Phrases: Handling Everyday Situations

Eksik bir şey var mı? (Ek-sik beer shey var mu?) - Is there anything missing?

Handy when checking if you have everything after a meal or while packing.

Yardım! (Yar-DUM) - Help!

In case you find yourself in need of assistance, this phrase will be your lifeline.

Expressions of Appreciation: Going Beyond Words

Güle güle kullanın. (Goo-leh goo-leh koo-lah-NEEN) - Use it with a smile. Commonly used when giving a gift, expressing the hope that the recipient will enjoy it.

Sağ olun. (Sah O-lun) - Thank you (more informal). A friendly way to express gratitude, especially when someone goes the extra mile.

Building Connections: Engaging Locals

Adınız nedir? (AH-duh-nuhz NEH-deer?) - What is your name? A friendly icebreaker to initiate conversations and make new friends.

Nasılsınız? (NAH-suhl-suhn-uhz) - How are you? Show genuine interest in the well-being of those you encounter on your journey.

As you weave these phrases into your interactions, let the language become a bridge, connecting you to the heart and soul of Istanbul. Whether you're strolling through historic neighborhoods or savoring Turkish delights, let your words echo the warmth and respect that define the cultural fabric of this enchanting city.

13.2 Maps and Navigation: Charting Your Course in Istanbul

Welcome to the mesmerizing maze of Istanbul, where every street tells a story, and every corner beckons with cultural treasures. This guide on maps and navigation equips you with the tools to not only explore the city's rich history but also navigate its bustling streets seamlessly. From ancient landmarks to hidden gems, these tips ensure you can confidently traverse Istanbul's diverse landscapes.

Visualize this: You, an intrepid adventurer, weaving through the city's tapestry armed with maps that unfold tales of the past and guide you to contemporary wonders. It's not just a guide; it's your cartographer's key to unlocking Istanbul's mysteries.

Digital Mapping: Your Modern-Day Compass

Google Maps: A reliable companion, Google Maps offers detailed insights into Istanbul's public transportation, walking routes, and real-time traffic updates. Download offline maps for areas with limited connectivity.

Yandex Maps: Especially useful in navigating Istanbul's intricate streets, Yandex Maps provides precise directions and incorporates local nuances seamlessly.

City Exploration Tips: Navigating Istanbul's Complex Terrain

Neighborhood Exploration: Istanbul is a city of neighborhoods, each with its own unique charm. Use maps to plan your day, focusing on specific areas like Sultanahmet, Beyoglu, or Kadikoy.

Landmarks as Anchors: Identify major landmarks on your maps, such as the Hagia Sophia, the Grand Bazaar, or the Bosphorus Bridge. These serve as visual anchors for orientation.

Public Transportation Guidance: Navigating the Commuter's Labyrinth

Transportation Hubs: Mark key transportation hubs on your map, including metro stations, tram stops, and ferry terminals. This ensures efficient and stress-free travel.

Walking Routes: Istanbul's charm lies in its walkable neighborhoods. Plan walking routes using maps, discovering hidden alleys, street art, and local cafes along the way.

Offline Map Downloads: Connectivity Anywhere, Anytime

Offline Maps: Download offline maps before venturing into areas with potentially limited connectivity. This guarantees access to navigation even when you're off the grid.

GPS Tracking: Ensure your device's GPS is enabled for precise location tracking. This is especially handy when exploring historic districts with narrow streets.

Language and Cultural Insights: Enhancing Your Experience

Cultural Landmarks: Identify cultural landmarks, museums, and historical sites on your maps to appreciate Istanbul's rich heritage. Learn about their significance before visiting.

Language Tips: Integrate basic Turkish phrases on your maps for quick reference, aiding interactions with locals and enhancing cultural immersion.

Local Advice: Seeking Authentic Experiences

Local Recommendations: Use maps to discover local recommendations for authentic dining experiences, hidden gems, and lesser-known attractions. Venture beyond the tourist hotspots.

Event Listings: Some mapping apps offer event listings. Check for local happenings, festivals, or exhibitions to add a dynamic layer to your exploration.

Navigating Istanbul is an art – a dance between tradition and modernity. With these mapping and navigation tips, you're not just traversing streets but unraveling stories, absorbing culture, and creating your unique narrative in this captivating city. Let your maps be your guide, and let Istanbul enchant you at every turn.

13.3 Recommended Reading: A Literary Journey through Istanbul's Soul

In the heart of Istanbul, where the Bosphorus whispers tales of the ages and minarets stand as silent storytellers, literature becomes a gateway to the city's soul. This guide on recommended reading is your literary compass, inviting you to delve into narratives that capture the essence of Istanbul. From timeless classics to contemporary gems, these books offer an immersive journey that goes beyond guidebooks and enriches your understanding of this enchanting metropolis.

Visualize this: You, an avid reader, wandering through Istanbul's streets with stories echoing in your mind, turning every corner into a chapter, and every café into a setting for tales untold. It's not just a guide; it's an invitation to explore Istanbul through the words of celebrated authors.

Timeless Classics: Unveiling Istanbul's Historical Layers

"My Name is Red" by Orhan Pamuk: A masterpiece by Nobel laureate Orhan Pamuk, this novel intricately weaves a tapestry of love, art, and mystery against the backdrop of the Ottoman Empire.

"Istanbul: Memories and the City" by Orhan Pamuk: Pamuk's memoir is a lyrical exploration of his relationship with Istanbul, blending personal anecdotes with the city's rich history.

Historical Fiction: Stories Set in Istanbul's Past

"The Architect's Apprentice" by Elif Shafak: Shafak takes you on a mesmerizing journey through Ottoman Istanbul, narrating the life of a young elephant keeper.

"The Janissary Tree" by Jason Goodwin: This historical mystery unfolds in 19th-century Istanbul, featuring the eunuch detective Yashim as he investigates a series of crimes.

Contemporary Tales: Istanbul in the Modern Era

"10 Minutes 38 Seconds in This Strange World" by Elif Shafak: Shafak's novel introduces you to the vibrant characters inhabiting Istanbul's margins, each with a captivating story to tell.

"The Museum of Innocence" by Orhan Pamuk: Pamuk's tale of love and obsession in Istanbul spans several decades, offering a poignant reflection on the city's social changes.

Culinary Journeys: Tasting Istanbul's Flavors Through Words

"Istanbul and Beyond: Exploring the Diverse Cuisines of Turkey" by Robyn Eckhardt: Discover the soul of Turkish cuisine through Eckhardt's culinary exploration, featuring recipes and stories from Istanbul and beyond.

Poetry and Prose: Capturing Istanbul's Essence

"Istanbul: A Tale of Three Cities" by Bettany Hughes: Hughes delves into Istanbul's layered history, presenting a vivid narrative that spans millennia and explores the city's multiple identities.

"Istanbul: City of Majesty at the Crossroads of the World" by Thomas F. Madden: A historical journey through the rise and fall of empires in Istanbul, highlighting its pivotal role as a crossroads of civilizations.

City Noir: Crime and Mystery in Istanbul

"The Bastard of Istanbul" by Elif Shafak: Shafak's novel blends family drama with political intrigue, set against the backdrop of Istanbul's complex history.

"The Snake Stone" by Jason Goodwin: Join detective Yashim as he unravels mysteries in 19th-century Istanbul, offering a gripping glimpse into the city's past.

Personal Reflections: Experiencing Istanbul Through Memoirs

"An Istanbul Anthology" by Kaya Genç: Genç curates a collection of essays and memoirs by various writers, offering diverse perspectives on Istanbul's charm and challenges.

Travel Essays: Navigating Istanbul's Streets in Words

"Istanbul: Memories of a City" by Orhan Pamuk: Pamuk's love letter to Istanbul combines memoir, travelogue, and cultural exploration, painting a multi-faceted portrait of the city.

"The Flea Palace" by Elif Shafak: Shafak's novel takes you into the lives of residents in an Istanbul apartment building, exploring the intricacies of their relationships and the city they call home.

These recommended readings invite you to embark on a literary odyssey through the streets of Istanbul, where every page unravels a layer of the city's history, culture, and soul. Let these books be your companions, offering insights and narratives that complement your physical journey through this timeless metropolis.

13.4 Glossary of Local Terms: Decoding Istanbul's Linguistic Tapestry

In the vibrant mosaic of Istanbul, language is a key to unlocking the city's cultural richness. This glossary of local terms is your linguistic companion, offering a glimpse into the unique vocabulary that colors daily life in this bustling metropolis. From culinary delights to friendly greetings, these terms will not only help you navigate Istanbul's streets but also connect with locals on a deeper level.

Visualize this: You, a linguistic explorer, weaving through Istanbul's markets and conversing with locals using phrases that resonate with the heartbeat of the city. It's not just a guide; it's your lexicon to decode Istanbul's linguistic tapestry.

Essential Greetings: Connecting with Warmth

Merhaba (mehr-HAH-bah): Hello - A warm and friendly greeting to start conversations with locals.

Günaydın (goo-NAH'YUH-duhn): Good morning - A polite way to wish someone a pleasant start to their day.

İyi günler (EE'YEE GOON'LEHR): Good day - A versatile greeting suitable for various times, wishing someone a good day ahead.

İyi akşamlar (EE'YEE AHK-SHAHM-LAHR): Good evening - Used in the later part of the day to greet people.

Hoş geldiniz (HOHSH GEHL-deen-EES): Welcome - A gracious expression used to welcome guests.

Culinary Delights: Exploring Turkish Flavors

Meze (MEH-zeh): A variety of small dishes served as appetizers, allowing you to savor a range of flavors in one sitting.

Kahvaltı (kah-VAHL-tuh): Breakfast - A hearty Turkish breakfast often includes cheese, olives, bread, and more.

Kahve (KAH-veh): Coffee - A beverage deeply ingrained in Turkish culture, available in various styles.

Çay (chai): Tea - A popular Turkish drink, typically served in small glasses, and an integral part of socializing.

Navigational Terms: Finding Your Way

Mahalle (mah-HAH-leh): Neighborhood - Istanbul is a city of diverse neighborhoods, each with its own character.

Caddesi (JAD-deh-see): Street - Commonly used in street names, helping you navigate the city's labyrinth.

Sokak (SOH-kahk): Alley - Narrow streets or alleys often leading to hidden gems.

Marketplace Lingo: Engaging in Bazaars

Pazar (pah-ZAHR): Market - Whether it's the Grand Bazaar or a local market, "pazar" is your gateway to vibrant shopping experiences.

Tane (TAH-neh): Piece - Useful when buying items by quantity, such as fruits, nuts, or spices.

Expressions of Appreciation: Gratitude in Turkish Style

Teşekkür ederim (teh-SHEHK-kur ed-AIR-im): Thank you - A polite way to express gratitude.

Çok güzel (chohk GOO-zel): Very beautiful - A compliment for something exceptionally beautiful or well-done.

Transportation Terms: Getting Around with Ease

Otobüs (OH-toh-boo): Bus - Istanbul's extensive bus network is a convenient way to navigate the city.

Vapur (vah-POOR): Ferry - Given Istanbul's unique location, ferries are a common mode of transport across the Bosphorus.

Time-Related Phrases: Embracing Turkish Rhythms

Saat kaç? (saht KAACH): What time is it? - Useful for keeping track of time and schedules.

Akşam (AHK-shahm): Evening - Used to refer to the evening or nighttime.

Learning and using these local terms will not only facilitate your practical needs but also enhance your overall experience by allowing you to connect with Istanbul's vibrant culture on a more intimate level. So, delve into this linguistic tapestry, embrace the richness of Turkish expressions, and let the city speak to you in its own words. Hoş geldiniz! (Welcome!)

Printed in Great Britain
by Amazon